Marketing Canada's Energy

Canada is heading for a crunch in its energy supply. On the one hand, while oil demand is decreasing, disappointing discovery and development trends indicate that oil imports will remain crucial to Canada throughout the 1980s. On the other hand, the international oil market will increasingly become a source of conflict over the next decade, as the USSR and its satellites seek to replace declining Soviet oil production, and the less developed countries raise their oil consumption. Added to this is the determination of the OPEC countries to ration out their reserves for maximum benefits, and the political volatility of the Persian Gulf region that supplies most Western oil imports.

Author I.A. McDougall shows that for an import-dependent country, Canada is ill-prepared for disruptions in its oil supply. He finds that the International Energy Agency and the National Energy Board cannot protect Canada's energy security, since control over oil imports is largely in the hands of international oil companies basing their decisions on corporate advantage. Moreover, the domestic production situation is jeopardized by the alienation of the oil-producing provinces, lowered energy investment expectations and a jumble of fiscal and tax expenditures.

McDougall asserts that the National Energy Program was a first step to forming an energy strategy independent of the major foreign-owned oil companies. But the creation of a National Energy Marketing Commission, with broad regulatory and purchasing powers, is needed to bring about a comprehensive energy management scheme.

I.A. McDougall is a professor at Osgoode Hall Law School. He has written extensively on energy issues.

Marketing Canada's Energy

The Canadian Institute for Economic Policy has been established to engage in public discussion of fiscal, industrial and other related public policies designed to strengthen Canada in a rapidly changing international environment.

The Institute fulfills this mandate by sponsoring and undertaking studies pertaining to the economy of Canada and disseminating such studies. Its intention is to contribute in an innovative way to the development of public policy in Canada.

Canadian Institute for Economic Policy
Suite 409, 350 Sparks St., Ottawa K1R 7S8

Marketing Canada's Energy

A Strategy for Security in Oil and Gas

I. A. McDougall

James Lorimer & Company, Publishers
in association with the
Canadian Institute for Economic Policy
Toronto 1983

ISBN 0-88862-590-1 cloth
ISBN 0-88862-589-8 paper

6 5 4 3 2 1   83 84 85 86 87 88

Canadian Cataloguing in Publication Data

McDougall, I.A., 1945-
  Marketing Canada's energy

1. Energy policy - Canada. I. Canadian Institute for Economic Policy. II. Title.

HD9502.C32M32   333.79′0971   C82-095319-9

Additional copies of this book
may be purchased from:

James Lorimer & Company, Publishers
Egerton Ryerson Memorial Building
35 Britain Street
Toronto, Ontario, M5A 1R7

Printed and bound in Canada

Contents

Tables and Figures

Foreword

Canadians are concerned about future energy supplies — particularly oil. The vagaries of the oil market have led the federal government to set in place the National Energy Program to guide future developments and protect the public interest.

Ian McDougall, however, writes that more than the existing controls will be needed to contend with the difficult energy problems ahead. His study urges the creation of a National Energy Marketing Commission that might develop durable solutions to our energy problems.

The institute believes that the merits of this concept should be publicly discussed and to this end is publishing this study. However, as with all our studies, the views expressed here are those of the author and do not necessarily reflect those of the institute.

Roger Voyer
Executive Director
Canadian Institute for Economic Policy

Preface

This analysis dwells on a number of quite rapidly moving targets. Begun in 1981, it was originally intended to be no more than a four- to five-month exercise, and involve a quick look at Canada's energy policy and the possible role of a National Marketing Plan. Since that time Canada has seen the emergence of a new National Energy Program, an agreement between Ottawa and Alberta over oil and gas pricing which may yet require revision, and the Constitutional Accord which may herald the evolution of wholesale constitutional amendment. To say that writing a book about all these subjects during the interim has been challenging would be a large, if not massive, understatement.

All of these changes have been the cause for significant frustration, and it has been necessary to maintain close, if not indeed intimate, monitoring of the areas that have been subject to such dramatic change. Nor have the challenges involved been confined to purely legislative regimes or legal agreements. In 1980-81 the international oil market was in turmoil and the prospects of significant shortages were likely in view of the revolution that had occurred in Iran and the war that later broke out between Iran and Iraq. Since this time Western economic recession, combined with upgraded Western industrial storage capacity, has eased what otherwise could have been a difficult downturn in the movement of international petroleum. Indeed the resilience of the consuming nations today has put OPEC on the defensive at least over the near term.

On the domestic front the National Energy Program (like the analysis that follows) took a somewhat dismal view of Canada's short-term energy-producing prospects. Recent activity on Canada's East Coast continental shelf has added a degree of support to the argument that Canada's long-term position as an oil producer may be better than initially supposed.

But for all the change and the somewhat brightened outlook, Canada's near-term prospects, as a hard issue of fact, are problematic. Canada's frontier projects involve very large logistical, technical, environmental and financial challenges in face of continued uncertainties. Its international import position remains hostage to long-term global demand and supply trends that are ominous despite a momentary reprieve. Moreover the NEP, while a major accomplishment, is but a first step which will not alone allow Canada to cope effectively with many of the development challenges ahead. More in the way of government action is necessary.

This analysis has deliberately assumed a pessimistic view of the country's short-run energy prospects. This view has not been taken with any pretensions of superior insight into what involves a range of highly problematic technical issues critical to a judgment about Canada's immediate position. It is a view that is based instead on historical fact; past mismanagement would suggest that, so far as Canada's remaining energy resources are concerned, pessimism has wisdom, if pessimism alone will temper caution in national energy development strategies. Certainly, defining a course on the basis of the worst assumptions about an apparently unpredictable state of affairs will provide more options. Canada has experienced tight imports, declining conventional oil production, rising import cost trends since 1973, and alarming disputes between Ottawa and the producing provinces. This study contains a number of suggestions about steps that might be taken to forearm Canada against an "unthinkable" series of occurrences that may further disrupt its energy balance.

The energy debate provides an illustration of the necessity of coming to terms with the limitations of a finite heritage of primary assets that can be economically developed. Provinces, acting independently in pursuit of development ambitions, often in rivalry with one another, work against effective national planning. Canada faces a neighbour which, despite short-term gluts, has a burgeoning appetite for raw resources. This country also faces an era of doubt about its domestic industrial potential. Recent estimates of Canada's energy capital needs suggest enormous challenges to be met if the necessary preliminary steps are taken to ensure that development proceeds in a fashion that will allow retention of a significant portion of the associated industrial opportunities. In this general regard, the discussion that follows examines what Canada might erect by way of regulatory structures both to protect its resource base and as a precursor to the implementation of national industrial strategies, based upon energy development over the next decade and more.

On the import side Canada needs more institutional expertise and a range of statutory powers that will support the implementation of import strategies that take into account variations within the overall international petroleum market. The creation of a specialized body is suggested for this reason, although its performance could of course usefully complement the other initiatives that are described.

On the domestic side it is suggested that the fiscal and regulatory complexities have not been fully rationalized. The effect of energy pricing upon the national fiscal balance, the limitations of Canada's existing emphasis upon petroleum and gas, and its general lack of forward regulatory control over energy development initiatives all conspire to reduce the total effectiveness of the statutory measures now in place. A series of broad changes is put forward that could significantly broaden the jurisdiction of the present National Energy Board, and the controls that govern the obtaining of capital market backing.

Ultimately, the core of the energy question rests on the issue of price. It is proposed that the present pricing controls be substantially broadened under the purview of a comprehensive national marketing plan which would administer an ongoing analysis of needs, development opportunities, market trends and federal-provincial revenue balances, and be applicable to all interprovincial and international transactions. It is argued that this step alone can lay to rest the many obstacles impeding development of energy resources in a manner that is, in practical terms, likely to prove of assistance to industry, the provinces and the public at large.

No analysis of this type can be produced without incurring very large debts. First, my thanks are owing to my research assistants, B. McCredy-Williams and Lynn Pillman. Some close friends have had to endure much talk, many questions and many "final drafts." I am indebted to all, most especially Bruce Willson, Professor Abraham Rotstein, and Roger Voyer of the Institute. In each instance they had highly useful suggestions to make, many of which were followed. Similar obligations are owing to Professors John Helliwell and Andrew Thompson of the University of British Columbia, Dean Stanley Beck, Professors Peter Cumming and Philip Anisman of Osgoode Hall Law School, and many others. It goes without saying that any liabilities for content are entirely mine.

Canadian Import Requirements and the International Petroleum Market

1

Canada's status as an oil producer has been in largely unrelenting decline for close to two decades. For this reason it is a speculative extreme to continue to assume the delineation and development of unknown petroleum supplies sufficient to provide even the depletion replacement[1] necessary to offset the decline of conventional production over the next decade. Even were one to begin with the presently unsupported assumption that such sources both exist and will be shortly discovered, the development and transportation logistics are alone apt to require a decade to resolve,[2] and costs by any standards will be extreme.[3] In the absence of such new sources of supply materializing unexpectedly, Canada must come to terms with the probability that present levels of petroleum consumption will only be maintained through large increases in petroleum imports.

A review of recent projections as to Canada's forward import needs firmly establishes two points. First, by most reasonable accounts, Canadian import needs will exhibit a steady upswing through the 1980s. Second, the level of uncertainty as to the ultimate extent of Canada's reliance upon imports is extreme. Variations in these estimates result principally from differing assumptions about undiscovered and/or untapped domestic sources of production, and the effects of conservation. Figure 1-1 illustrates the wide divergence of informed opinion in this regard. The extreme estimates are those of Dome Petroleum as quoted by the *International Petroleum Encyclopaedia* of 1978.[4] The Dome "worst case" projection reflected the degree of Canada's import needs without either significant conservation or tarsands production investment over the forecast period 1980-95. The Dome "best case" by way of contrast assumed both.

The National Energy Board's (NEB) 1978 analysis[5] offered an enormously more optimistic outlook. But the validity of this optimism was rather dubious by virtue of the incorporation of equally enormous

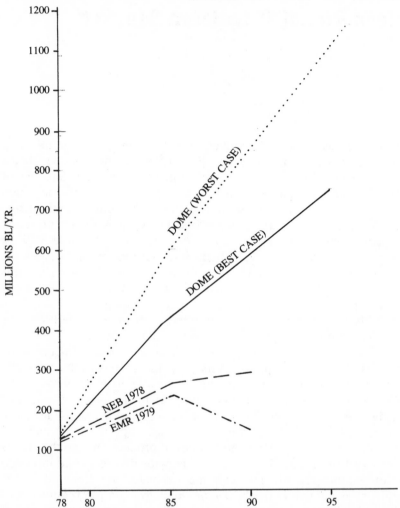

FIGURE 1-1
CANADIAN PETROLEUM NET IMPORT REQUIREMENTS,
1978-95

and unrealistic assumptions, including, among other things, import costs of between $17-18 per barrel, an optimistic view of Canadian economic performance over the forecast period, and the timely approval, commencement and completion of the now much-delayed Alsands and Cold Lake synthetic plants and of the Dempster Lateral to the Alaska Highway Natural Gas Pipeline project.

The estimates of Energy, Mines and Resources Canada (EMR)[6] were an attempt at updating the NEB projections in light of apparent errors in the board's initial assumptions. The perhaps remarkable downward trends in demand, particularly past the year 1985, once again, like the earlier NEB figures, depended upon optimistic assumptions with respect to both domestic and international prices, minimal market impediments to large-scale natural gas penetration in the Central and Atlantic regions, and few constraints deterring major and sustained levels of investment in new conventional, frontier and synthetic production over the forecast period.

There are innumerable estimates available from both industry and government sources that suggest different scenarios. Gulf Canada, for example, has been quoted as estimating Canadian needs to hover in the 190 million barrels per year range from the 1980s through 1995. EMR even conducted one analysis that produced an import dependency of only 730,000 barrels a year by 1995! On the other hand, official presentations by Canadian representatives to the International Energy Agency (IEA) have reflected a substantially less optimistic view than the EMR figures represented in Figure 1-1.[7]

These variations evidence a disconcertingly high degree of uncertainty about future Canadian import needs, even in the face of often highly restrictive assumptions over price and supply stability within the international market. In view of so large a divergence of informed opinion, the adoption of import strategies that assume the worst of an at best poor situation — in particular, increasing import reliance — may be prudent. A careful survey of the major danger points that can affect the status of international petroleum flows and market prices should be conducted with the objective of identifying mitigation and/or preventative strategies that might be available.

The apparent inevitability of increased import reliance over the near term raises at least three vital practical issues:

- How probable is it that the international market will remain stable during the next decade?
- If international petroleum supplies become short, will Canada be able to fall back upon any international commitments to apportion shortages among the major import-consumers?
- Can Canada financially manage the large foreign exchange pressures brought about by higher levels of import dependency?

Each of these issues is discussed in the pages that follow.

3

Imports and the Security of Supply

Where options have existed, most Western consuming nations have historically preferred to limit their exposure to the effects of disruptions in the international petroleum market by developing their indigenous potential.[8] Canada has been no exception. The possibility of import interruptions was a major catalyst in the promotion of western field expansion in the early 1950s when it became apparent that Canada might possess potentially significant quantities of producible petroleum.[9]

Canadian interest was also prompted by financial and tactical considerations. The possibility of large-scale gas and oil exports to the U.S. offered a series of advantages. The addition of the larger markets created an opportunity for rapid production expansion at a rate far beyond that which the domestic market alone could justify.[10] The inflow of foreign exchange that resulted was considered of substantial, if not crucial, importance to the country's balance of trade with the U.S. Moreover, the creation of a complex of overland pipelines offered a measure of defensive security that was not true of otherwise cost-efficient but vulnerable sea-going tankers.[11] Other factors should also be noted for their bearing upon Canadian policies, including encouraging the growth of Canadian industrial and residential markets for specifically designated fuels such as natural gas, and increased employment in the western provinces. But the ultimate goal of "domestic production self-sufficiency" was primarily born from concern about future international conflict rather than a hard evaluation of various cost-efficient choices.

The prospects of Middle East instability in mid 1982 were not less than they were three decades ago. But the nature of the threat has altered. In the 1950s the main risk lay with potential transportation disruptions[12] rather than large-scale production stoppages or arbitrary price hikes. While the latter were not unheard of, a producer-cartel remained a distant and "improbable" development. Most of the crucial decisions from the wellhead to the burner tips of Europe and North America were still effectively under the control of the major international oil giants.[13] And while the so-called "Seven Sisters" were a formidable cartel in their own right,[14] they had no collective interest in shaking the financial and economic roots of the Western economies.[15] The early concern of the importing nations lay primarily with Egypt and the possible closure of the Suez Canal, and less with the dangers of an oil company cartel or the policies of the oil-producing states.

4

Most oil carriage during the 1950s and 1960s was via "small" tankers for whom the closure of the Suez Canal was a serious matter adding thousands of miles to the distance over which crude oil would have to be carried.[16] For this reason Egyptian affairs remained the pre-eminent variable influencing the reliability of Middle Eastern crude supplies, and the country's stature amongst both consuming and producing nations was for this same reason at something of an historical zenith.

In 1983 the world still labours under the ominous shadow of any one of several Middle Eastern conflicts developing into large-scale war. As one writer somewhat cryptically observed:

> . . . 13 of the present Arab heads of state, or more than half of them, have reached power by forcibly removing their predecessors in one way or another; and in the past 15 years Arabs have fought Arabs in 12 fierce wars. This is the area on which, for better or worse, we depend on stable oil supplies.[17]

Transportation routes and the status of the Suez Canal are no longer of paramount concern. The emergence of the VLCC (Very Large Crude Carrier) and the ULCC (Ultra Large Crude Carrier)[18] has made even an expanded Suez redundant for all but a small percentage of world tanker flows.[19] Egypt is still in a position of influence as a large military force altogether capable of destabilizing Middle Eastern affairs. But its influence is far from pivotal. Egypt's status very much depends upon the continued economic and political support of a number of large Arab producing states, most notably the Kingdom of Saudi Arabia,[20] as well as the United States.

It might be said that the period during which the status of Suez was of major importance represented the first phase of a still-evolving process. The second phase began in 1961 with the formation of the Organization of Petroleum Exporting Countries (OPEC).[21] From 1961 to 1980 power began to shift, initially by slow degrees, in favour of the individual producing states at the expense of all of the other actors, including Egypt, the major oil companies, and the consuming nations. The history of this shift in the balance of Middle Eastern power, and its more prominent episodes such as the Anglo-Iranian oil dispute, the Exxon drops in the posted price, and the 1967 and 1973 oil embargoes and price hikes, are by now all well chronicled[22] and, with one exception, will not be laboured here. The exception concerns OPEC and the credit usually given to it as the pivotal instrument controlling both the shape and pace of events in the Middle East. As a result of this initial assumption, much speculation has focused upon the implications of OPEC's possible demise with respect to the price of oil in the international market. While theorizing of this sort has sold much journalistic copy, it may obscure more than it reveals about current Middle East reality. Foremost is a misapprehension about the governing trends, both historical and contemporary, of the region's oil politics generally, and OPEC's institutional tenure in particular.[23]

OPEC is most usually referred to as a cartel.[24] It owes its existence to the express aim of its members to coordinate producer policy.[25] But from time to time its major preoccupations have ranged over such topics as too little oil, too much oil, balancing heavy and light grade production, too high prices, too low prices, regional political turmoil, the political policies of destination countries, assistance to the underdeveloped nations, the balance of regional military power, and so on. OPEC's very existence has been jeopardized by internal rivalries, competitive undercutting between members with the multinationals, binding state-to-state commitments between producing and consuming nations, manipulation of crude output levels by individual members to influence the strength of the spot market, wars, and irreconcilable differences over pricing policies.[26] While OPEC may indeed be a cartel, it is one whose behaviour defies textbook definition. It is not guided by any single all-prevalent interest such as profit maximization. Its historical existence has been tenuous, its motives mixed, and its influence as the single most effective agent of higher prices vastly exaggerated.

Undoubtedly, OPEC will at some point disappear either through displacement by a more elaborate institution for political and economic dialogue between its members, or through a complete break in communications and eventual abandonment. But it would be highly unrealistic to assume that its breakup will have a durable impact upon the overall direction of the world oil market which will be governed in the long run by fundamentally declining global production prospects and enlarging global requirements.

Despite the favourable market conditions of mid 1982 we are probably entering a third phase in the history of Middle Eastern oil affairs — namely, an era of supply-preoccupied markets with more or less unlimited willingness to absorb all available production. If this reality begins to dominate world trade, the predominant medium of exchange will shift in favour of the spot market at the expense of the presently more important contract market.[27] In this market environment OPEC will be less able to claim credit for holding up the market price,[28] and its present membership will feel less obligated towards its maintenance. If world economic conditions improve, the unchecked growth in demand in the traditional market areas should be sufficient to support the adjustments to crude oil prices necessary to keep them ahead of the rate of inflation, thus allowing expanding real returns to producing nations that are able and remain willing to sell.[29]

But it is becoming increasingly likely that a gap between the West's petroleum requirements and what is currently "OPEC production"[30] will develop in the late 1980s and continue thereafter. This trend can be attributed to four fundamental realities that will govern conditions in the international market for the next decade or more. These are (1) the growth of Western import needs, (2) the increasing global demand for oil, (3) the instability of present sources of supply, and (4) the constraints against coordinated action among consuming nations.

The Growth of Western Import Needs

Recent IEA and OECD analysis suggests sustained import demand from the Western industrial economies over the next decade. These estimates when compared with others such as Exxon Corporation's most recent figures published in its *World Energy Outlook*[31] reveal some debate as to rates of increases in aggregate requirements of the Western consuming regions. But most analyses clearly indicate substantial and sustained crude import reliance, despite brave commitments by the nations concerned to fuel substitution programs, massive consumer conservation efforts, anticipated reductions in the rates of population growth, and lowered economic performance.[32]

As is true of all projections of this nature, significant *ceteris paribus* assumptions were employed. Full-scale economic depression, which would undoubtedly accompany any substantial long-term disruption of international petroleum flows, was put aside for the purposes of generating most probable demand patterns, as was the possibility of large-scale military hostilities embroiling any number of the nations surveyed. There is of course no doubt that either eventuality would produce a dramatic change in the accuracy of the estimates. Indeed, as discussed below, the overwhelming weight of available evidence clearly suggests some improbability that Western requirements will continue to be fully met much beyond 1990. Given that there is no risk of more being consumed than the quantity at any one moment available, the likelihood of a deterioration of the very conditions assumed stable for the purposes of the estimates after 1990 would seem to be more or less guaranteed.

7

Increasing Global Demand for Oil

If one assumes that traditional Western market requirements can be met for the next two decades, it is still necessary to face the probability of large new competitive pressures for available world petroleum from two sources: the USSR and the Less Developed Countries (LDCs).

The Soviet Union

At the time of writing, the USSR retains the distinction of being the world's largest oil producer.[33] By any estimate the country possesses enormous reserves of both petroleum and natural gas.[34] These reserves continue to play a vital role in the Soviet economy's pre-eminence in the socialist world. Oil and gas exports reportedly account for a full 60 per cent of the USSR's annual foreign exchange earnings.[35] Of particular importance are the current sales of gas and oil to Austria, Italy and West Germany.[36] From these expanding markets the USSR obtains substantial credit with which it can purchase much needed industrial and technical equipment from the West, a not inconsiderable percentage of which involves equipment related to the oil and gas industry.[37] Oil and gas exports also have a major stabilizing influence upon the Warsaw bloc. Most of the member nations lack significant indigenous sources of supply and rely heavily upon the USSR.[38] Should supplies from the Middle East become tight, the political and strategic value of Soviet oil within the Warsaw bloc will be even greater if production can be maintained and costs held within tolerable limits.

Soviet oil prospects have been the subject of much recent controversy. A growing number of authorities believe that the Soviet Union will be unable to hold the line on present production targets. It has been suggested that USSR production will have peaked between 1981 and 1984 and that protracted shortages will develop and persist for the next decade if not longer.[39]

It is difficult to avoid noting disquieting similarities between the Soviet and Canadian predicaments. Both nations share inhospitable climates, large transportation barriers, and high industrial expectations, which make adequate petroleum supplies one of the most fundamental cornerstones of future prosperity. Both nations have vast areas of potential that deserve concentrated exploration. In both countries the rate of discovery and development of new supplies from these "frontier areas" appears to have lagged behind the rate required to offset conventional depletion. In both cases large export "commitments" (albeit commitments made under substantially different

8

circumstances) have led to depletion rates that have accelerated the need to find and develop new sources. This is a task of such urgency that it is almost impossible to give priority to frontier transportation and development investment decisions so as to make best use of the available prospects. And finally, over the near term both countries may have to contend with the ever-present likelihood of large-scale prospective shortages and further cost increases which have already begun to impact upon the two economies.[40]

There are of course unique aspects to the Soviet dilemma. Western intelligence sources[41] suggest that ambitious Soviet production targets have been responsible for an overemphasis upon infill drilling and tertiary recovery techniques,[42] which has in turn resulted in large-scale production difficulties, past (and prospective) acceleration in field development investment levels, and a starvation of labour and capital flows into the exploration and development sectors. There are additional considerations which explain the reported slowness of the USSR to come to terms with an evidently looming crisis, the major one being deficient domestic technology. Soviet rigs are reputed to be less productive than comparable Western equipment due to both the unreliable nature of the prevalent motive power systems (direct drive turbines as opposed to rotary types with conventional piston engines), the quality of the metallurgy (which affects size, complexity, weight and reliability of both rigs and, most importantly, drill stems), and the limited experience and/or proficiency of Soviet drilling crews.[43] U.S. 1978 estimates placed overall Soviet drilling performance at about one-fifth that of the American industry with a comparable number of rigs in operation.[44]

Moreover, the institutional shape of the Soviet regulatory system appears to have laboured under important defects, primarily the overemphasis upon ever-increasing production targets. Suffice it to say that a well-defined demarcation between the jurisdiction of field conservation authorities and production-oriented elements in the economy, be the economic system capitalist, socialist or communist, has advantages that have proven lacking in the USSR.[45]

From the Soviet point of view the crude oil problem may yet be reduced to a basic question: Is it easier to develop or import the technology necessary to undertake a massive exploration, development and transportation program than to secure a greater share of production from already established Middle East sources? While the analysis of an issue of such scope embraces complexities of judgment beyond the purview of this study, it appears difficult to escape the conclusion that

9

Soviet pressure for a higher percentage of current import supplies of petroleum will very probably increase during the latter part of the decade, be that pressure in the form of another very large buyer in the marketplace, massive diplomatic effort in Middle East affairs, or unrestrained force of arms.

Nor is the Soviet Union a stranger to the international energy market. Historically the USSR has imported large quantities of Iranian gas[46] which, through displacement of indigenous Soviet production, permitted highly remunerative gas sales to Western Europe. But the productivity of these exports completely depended upon both the price charged by Iran,[47] and the ability of the USSR to pass on any cost increases under the governing contracts of sale to its Western customers. Before the overthrow of the late Shah gas prices had begun to rise sharply. Since then protracted negotiations and service interruptions have made the future status of Iranian exports somewhat problematic. This uncertainty was of course increased with the outbreak of Iranian-Iraqi hostilities. But the overall implications are clear for the Soviet Union. Without reliable gas imports, gas exports to Western Europe represent a strain on the Soviet energy system, necessitating more gas development costs. Higher Iranian border prices were a direct "bite" out of the net foreign exchange earning potential of gas exports to Western Europe. On balance, large Soviet gas potential and substantial foreign exchange needs make reduced gas supplies to Europe improbable so long as some net return is possible. But a protracted closure of Iranian imports might direct activities towards expanding short-term Soviet natural gas production — activities which, under the best of circumstances, might be better applied towards oil discovery to offset the projected petroleum shortfalls.

In short, while the Soviets possess abundant natural gas, their petroleum outlook is widely believed to be highly tenuous for the next decade and beyond. The country's frontier prospects have yet to materialize. Its current sources have in some cases experienced, and in other cases are on the verge of experiencing, sharp production declines. Petroleum and natural gas export sales to the West are the Soviet Union's largest single source of foreign purchasing power, and yet the country has a large materially-expectant population which may not be prepared to accept widespread domestic shortages and/or higher costs. For these reasons a large Soviet presence in Middle East affairs and an increasing Soviet reliance upon the region's petroleum production would seem to be highly probable.[48]

The Less Developed Countries

A second major source that may materially add to the strains upon future international crude supplies will come from the Less Developed Countries (LDCs). Most of these nations have expansive industrial ambitions which will entail higher levels of energy consumption. Obviously, a precise estimate of the growth of LDCs' requirements is highly speculative, but given the vast populations involved, relatively minor increases in per capita consumption will dramatically impact on the petroleum import supply picture worldwide.[49]

OPEC has long been preoccupied with the capacity of the LDCs to absorb the sharp increases to the posted crude price. To some extent LDCs have received preferential treatment in the allocation of contract oil, a percentage of which has reportedly often found its way into spot market commerce.[50] As an "indirect subsidy" or transfer payment, such supplies have represented a large gain for the LDCs involved. But issues that remain unresolved include the degree to which priority will continue to be extended by OPEC to the needs of such countries as they expand, and the supply implications for the oil-hungry Western economies, which will bear the full weight of future shortfalls should preference be given to the less developed world.

One recent survey[51] suggested that the LDCs not only represent the major source of energy consumption growth for the balance of this century, but also are ultimately going to depend more upon Western energy technology to keep pace with indigenous requirements than upon direct importation of either energy or fuels such as oil or gas. In this regard, circumstances of individual nations vary considerably. The People's Republic of China, for example, is believed to have substantial unexplored and undeveloped petroleum producing potential, particularly in the environmentally harsh Tsaidam Basin region.[52] A transfer of Western technology, including the use of Landsat[53] and EROS data to locate areas of highest potential, is in progress. In other countries, indigenous petroleum and gas production prospects are low to non-existent, thus increasing reliance upon thermal, hydroelectric or nuclear technology as the long-term solution. In both situations there is scope for productive cooperation between technically advanced nations and LDCs in the search for large-scale energy sources over the long term. But in the course of the forthcoming decade, heated controversies over the distribution of conventional fuel supplies between the developed and undeveloped worlds may develop, and there is every likelihood that import flows to Western Europe and North America will be constrained as a result.

11

Future OPEC Import Flows

There is no reason for optimism about the future reliability of OPEC import supplies. As noted above, it seems clear that both Canadian and U.S. near-term import exposure may again be increasing.[54] A careful evaluation of the risks and strategies that might be implemented to mitigate the consequences of large-scale future disruptions is perhaps overdue for this reason.

There are (at least) five major peacetime factors that could lead any of the producing nations to reduce output, thereby lessening Canadian import access (directly or indirectly). These factors are summarized below:

Limited Domestic Development Prospects

Limited power to recycle foreign currency via the purchase of Western goods and services is a factor that bears a close relationship to the surplus of currencies discussed below. However, even where a producing country is prepared to sell,[55] the flow of foreign buying power may well represent little, if any, real gain over the short and possibly medium terms. Too rapid attempts at modernization can create enormous social and political upheavals, the case of Iran being the most dramatic and current example. There are, however, other instances, most notably Iraq and Saudi Arabia,[56] where there appears to exist very real concern that the drive towards modernization may so strain the social fabric as to lead to civil dissent. A necessary result of reduced domestic investment might well be an expansion of the already protracted trade imbalances.[57]

Foreign Exchange Surpluses

The accumulation of an excess of foreign exchange might lead a producing nation to reduce petroleum output. The reasoning underlying such a decision is quite simple. Inflationary pressures have caused most Western currencies to depreciate rapidly. On the other hand, oil held in the ground is an appreciating asset requiring none of the managerial and investment sophistication necessary for the administration of foreign currency holdings. Deferred production would thus be a logical choice. From the point of view of other members of OPEC anxious to sell more oil, such production restraints by one or more of the larger sellers would be popularly received as a welcome stiffening force in the market.

Nor is this possibility historically without precedent. Recent Saudi investment programs in production capacity have followed a timetable which is considerably below peak potential. This decision has repeatedly been explained as in part the result of the greater value of oil as against yet more foreign currency.[58]

Armament Sales

The role of military arms sales as a trade item may prove insufficient in the future to offset developing foreign currency imbalances. As an initial matter, resumed Japanese interest in armament production carries with it the likelihood of intense competition between the Western armament dealers. But at a certain point there are strategic dangers in delivery of ever more sophisticated arms technology to the oil-producing countries. Even today some of the Middle East's military hardware is but a short step below the current equipment in use by the superpowers. Further "arms recycling" is both inadvised and improbable, and continued sales of existing types are limited by the productivity of the training programs in progress and the rate at which such hardware depreciates.

The arms trade represents a great temptation both because of the potentially enormous profits involved and the desire of the Western nations to establish secure sources of oil supply. The sale of advanced weapons is a virtual guarantee of ongoing economic relations with the country concerned because of the need for parts, training, and operating/service facilities.[59] From the perspective of the producing nations, long-term oil supply agreements are an important lever which has already been employed to secure advanced weapons technology. The recent embargo imposed by Libya against India[60] and the later arrangements made with Pakistan with respect to nuclear enrichment technology in exchange for loans and secure oil are an important and frightening case in point.

In brief, the total value of Middle East arms purchases is limited by the reluctance of Western suppliers to provide the latest generation of superweapons, and the limited speed with which qualified handlers of such equipment can be trained in any case. Thus future sales to "friendly" oil producers may not have much impact with respect to petroleum supply agreements in the near future. In still other cases, producing nations could in future resort to production reductions or embargoes in an attempt to secure weapons. And finally, the presence of large quantities of sophisticated weaponry, in the Middle East particularly, heightens the probability of any one of a series of regional rivalries and squabbles escalating into conflict of a sufficient scale to disrupt oil traffic over a large area. The Iraqi-Iranian war represented the realization of but one of a series of potential conflicts.

13

Reserve Life Indices

While the current worldwide surplus has created difficult revenue adjustments for many producers, concern over reserve life indices has created a degree of apprehension in many countries. In the case of Venezuela, historically Canada's largest single source of imported oil, declines in the reserve life index have resulted in reductions in annual deliveries.[61] As noted above, the Saudis have expressed similar concerns, notwithstanding the relative enormity of that country's petroleum reserves.[62] Other producing nations have likewise debated production levels in face of declining life indices and controversy about the total remaining recoverable reserves. Kuwait and Oman are two cases in point.[63] The drilling, marketing and secondary processing programs under way in Iran immediately prior to the Revolution[64] were a reflection of concern about the long-term future of that nation as an oil exporter, and the need to establish a secondary economic base.

Many of the Middle Eastern producers appear to recognize that, after oil exhaustion has set in, domestic economic growth prospects are marginal if not perhaps non-existent. For this reason, oil production will undoubtedly be subjected to ever more careful control to ensure that this limited form of wealth can be tapped to its fullest potential in terms of long-term purchasing power. Until recently most field production decisions were made by the major international oil companies with little input from the producing governments.[65] Indeed the major constraint on production extended not from good conservation practices in a field management sense, or even long-term national economic planning objectives, but from variations in the absorption capacities of the international market from time to time.[66] Now, however, that the producing countries have started to assume responsibility for production management through regulation and state petroleum corporations, an overwhelming alteration in their perspective appears to have emerged. Where before many of these countries were apprehensive that production was being artificially restrained by the oil majors, some producers are now beginning to regulate production levels around the maintenance of an optimal rate life index. Short-run output and revenue maximization constrained only by the world's market requirements will become increasingly a thing of the past following an industrial recovery and an end to the current surplus capacity of the producing countries.

East-West Rivalry

Fundamental realignments with respect to the Eastern and Western blocs will likely precipitate changes in the pattern of petroleum trade.

As noted above, prospective production declines in the USSR will continue to animate Soviet interest and involvement. Moreover, the impact of the Iraqi-Iranian conflict upon Soviet access to Iranian gas supplies and, in the long term, its share of future Iraqi petroleum is problematic. Seven Eastern European communist countries were drawing approximately 400,000 barrels a day from Iran and Iraq prior to the war. This has all but stopped and represents an immediate cut of 20 per cent in the amount of oil absorbed under ordinary circumstances by the seven countries concerned.[67] The ultimate capacity of the USSR to divert domestic production away from either Soviet or Western import customers in favour of its satellites is a matter of speculation. If nothing else, it is clear the stakes of the East bloc in Middle Eastern affairs have risen dramatically. Nor is this the product of ideological compulsion as much as it is the result of the selfsame economic pressures that have so tied the Western nations to reliance upon this region. Under such circumstances to expect anything less than increasingly intense Eastern bloc competition in virtually every sphere of Middle Eastern affairs would be ill-advised.

The above factors share a single common denominator: the future availability of international oil, so far as it continues to be dominated by the current OPEC producers, is likely to be problematic over the forthcoming decade. It is a matter of some concern that Canada, as an import-reliant nation, should do whatever it can to offset the consequences that otherwise may result from a tightened supply situation.

The International Energy Agency
Canada, as a member of the International Energy Agency, is committed to the IEA's major objectives which include the promotion of "secure oil supplies on reasonable and equitable terms,"[68] the development of "common effective measures to meet oil supply emergencies by developing an emergency self-sufficiency in oil supplies, restraining demand and allocating available oil among . . . countries on an equitable basis,"[69] and the establishment of an international bureaucracy to administer the measures agreed by the IEA's members.[70]

The IEA's tangible accomplishments to date include the development of higher levels of storage capacity in the member states, with reserves on hand sufficient to last 90 days,[71] the preparation of contingent oil demand restraint programs effective to depress

15

consumption by as much as 10 per cent,[72] and the emergency allocation of international supplies whenever the signatory nations,[73] or any individual nation,[74] are forced to sustain a reduction in supplies in excess of 7 per cent of the average daily final consumption rate.

The creation of the IEA was a difficult[75] and desirable objective. But it has not become a major countervailing force that the import-consuming nations can rely upon for long-term protection from the effects of coordinated producer action. In reality, the IEA is little more than a first, albeit necessary, step that labours under significant limitations.

First among the IEA's weaknesses is the fact that the emergency allocation mechanism will not cut in until supplies are reduced by more than 7 per cent. Experience has already demonstrated that a much smaller shortfall of between 2 to 3 per cent can touch off a price explosion in the spot market, with the inevitable increase in the posted prices of OPEC ultimately following.[76] If the shortfalls are unevenly allocated amongst member nations, the adverse effect on spot market transactions may prove to be disproportionately high. A 2 per cent reduction of U.S. imports expressed in barrels is a vastly larger figure than the equivalent percentage of the oil imports of the Grand Duchy of Luxembourg. If this unevenness is further complicated by a 6 per cent reduction in the supplies destined for a large consuming nation like Japan or West Germany or the U.S., as opposed to a 1 or 2 per cent reduction in oil flows to Sweden or Switzerland, the impact upon spot prices may prove devastating. To this extent, IEA reliance upon straight percentages fails to cope effectively with the spot market as the principal agent of higher international oil prices.

A second defect of the IEA Agreement lies in its failure to provide for an enforcement mechanism. The system is ultimately dependent upon the goodwill of the signatory nations until such time as formal sanctions are incorporated.

Third, the IEA cannot claim any major accomplishments in the establishment of firm conservation programs. The recent declaration of an overall import reduction of 5 per cent was nothing more than a voluntary guideline with no firm commitments to specific conservation programs being assumed by any of the IEA membership. Indeed, the reduction target was to be achieved without a lessening of the economic performances of the nations concerned. In fact, import levels actually experienced tended to track economic declines, while those nations whose economies remained buoyant proved to be far less successful.[77]

16

Fourth, the IEA Agreement masks very real differences in philosophy within its membership. Some hold the view that imports should be pooled under the umbrella of a single coordinated agency which should then allocate supplies to the member nations. Others, including particularly West Germany and Japan, place more faith in the market system and the role of higher prices as a conservation incentive. This view fails to account for a number of factors, including some evidence of price inelasticity in the short run. As one commentator noted:

> In the short run, demand is only price inelastic, and supply is no longer determined predominantly by economic considerations, but rather by the production policies of OPEC members. As a matter of fact, higher spot-market prices will not only lead to higher OPEC prices, as has already happened, but might also induce OPEC countries to lower production while increasing their total oil revenues at the same time. And higher prices in any one importing country will only have the suction-like effect of pulling away supplies destined for other countries. In the absence of a system of fair distribution of oil among all countries, those nations that follow the market approach in bidding for oil may force other countries to match their higher prices.[78]

In short, the IEA includes member nations that materially contribute to the difficulties with respect to import supply security and international price increases that led to its creation in the first instance. The differences between the member states with respect to such issues as pricing and conservation, and the proper scope of the agency to coordinate import purchasing, would seem at this time to preordain limited success in the future.

Notably, the IEA does not include a number of large import-consuming nations. From the Western bloc the most notable exclusion is France, whose purchasing decisions often seem based on a naked attempt to secure maximum domestic advantage, regardless of the consequences. Other nations outside of the Western bloc have not been invited to join as a matter of policy. As noted above, the future needs of both the less developed world and the Warsaw Pact nations may ultimately reduce the already limited effectiveness of the IEA as an agent of stability.

Indeed the failure to include all of the world's major import consumers is not the only IEA shortcoming. No provision appears to have been made for the role of major international oil companies. Canada has had direct experience that suggests this may be the source of future difficulty. In 1978, Canada was offered a foretaste of the so-called "quota system" of the IEA in operation. Imperial Oil attempted to justify a diversion of Venezuelan crude during the Iranian crisis on the claim that the reduction was based solely on rules established by the International Energy Agency. The company's corporate manager[79] was quoted by the Toronto *Globe and Mail* as having said that: "[Exxon Corporation of New York] decided not to play God (in the reallocation of oil worldwide) and simply decided to use the agreed on formula."[80] On the basis of this logic, Imperial announced a diversion to U.S. markets of 25,000 barrels a day of Venezuelan crude, which amounted to 25 per cent of Imperial's Maritime and Quebec imports, and 5 per cent of total Canadian imports for the same region.

The Imperial argument was an elaborate attempt to justify the imposition of the maximum burden on Canada, and was in fact completely unrelated to the IEA allocation formula which had not been invoked. The IEA system could only be triggered by the member nations, either collectively or individually. There was, and is, no mechanism for an international oil company to initiate the process. Moreover, in this case Imperial was prepared, through its own supply commitments, to reduce Canada's total import flows to the 5 per cent limit without ever considering the consequences for Canada if other companies supplying the same market region had problems. Canada at the time had been in receipt of some 40,000 barrels a day from Iran supplied by Gulf and others. The revolutionary turmoil effectively put a stop to these exports, and Canada ran the risk of substantial supply difficulties as a direct consequence. The Imperial action to reduce non-Iranian supplies only served to further burden Canada's strained import position.

But this experience dramatically underscored another major weakness of the IEA Agreement. The major oil giants still effectively control the transportation and marketing of most of the world's oil supply and yet remain beyond the effective control of the IEA members. They exert enormous control over the allocation of international oil, with such decisions based on their individual assessments of corporate advantage. Given this to be the case, Canada should not place too much reliance upon the IEA as a means of securing stability within the international market, without making some effort to bring the majors to heel.

In brief, the IEA Agreement represents a limited accomplishment at most with respect to the control of international oil. Its allocation formula begins to operate only in face of large import flow reductions and does nothing to assist small volume changes which can substantially distort the international price structures. There is no formal enforcement mechanism, no firm commitment as to specific energy-saving programs, and no agreement among the membership to coordinate international oil purchases. Finally, even assuming a willingness of the member states to act together under distress circumstances, significant oil-consuming nations are not party to the agreement and the major oil companies are not controlled by it. It is but a beginning.

Import Supply Regulation: Summary and Recommendations

It is difficult to make a confident assessment of world petroleum traffic. Even short-term predictions are frequently frustrated by non-market variables. Prior to the Iraqi-Iranian hostilities, the spot market was in a borderline glut and the 1980-81 winter supply prospects appeared solid. The war temporarily clouded this outlook but, through a combination of storage drawdowns and higher production levels in some of the OPEC and non-OPEC states, shortages and a "hotter" spot market were averted. More than a few authoritative analysts, however, were predicting major supply shortfalls into the summer of 1981 and thereafter due to reduced Western storage levels, expanding worldwide import needs, and changing OPEC production patterns. Not only did these changes not occur, but 1982 appeared to promise unprecedented international crude surpluses, with some researchers projecting a persistence of soft market conditions until the end of the decade.

While there can be no real doubt that there is a current excess of production capacity, it is a surplus that is measured against the demands of Western industrial economies in steep recession. The consequential downward pressure on the world crude oil price has served only to further devastate the grounding economics of alternative energy developments, both in Canada (where ironically they represent what may be the most promising route to economic recovery) and worldwide. And this of course appears to advance the probability of fundamental demand and supply imbalances in future for which we will be largely unprepared.

Thus, even if a higher degree of military and political stability than the facts warrant is assumed in the Middle East, the long-term outlook must still be termed bleak if economic recovery and development of major new sources of supply and/or massive conservation do not occur.

Despite perhaps the best efforts of the import-consuming nations, demands have proven hard to moderate independent of economic performance. World supply prospects have not improved. Production costs from new sources have been increasing and prices will have to rise in an effort to offset future market imbalances. For these reasons, any domestic energy strategy that assumes a long-term free availability of international petroleum is ill-advised.

As of 1982 Canada was exposed, given its current levels of import reliance. Disappointing domestic discovery and development trends of the past decade would appear to have condemned the country to more rather than less import dependence in the near future. And it yet remains a possibility that significantly higher levels of domestic self-reliance will prove so costly an achievement that, even at substantially higher prices, offshore imports might remain a comparatively more attractive alternative from a cost point of view for some time.

Cost projection, however, remains every bit as risky and uncertain an exercise as supply tracking. The very factors that suggest import supplies are unstable argue equally in favour of sharp price increases in the international market. In Canada's case there is value in cautious pessimism in attempting to predict the trends of the world market in the future. Past analysis was so tainted by unwarranted optimism and sloppy research that it proved more damaging than useful to domestic energy policy-making.[81] Fortunately, Canada was able to fall back on oil producibility surpluses. As a result, the otherwise damaging effects of the changing price conditions in the world market could be held to a minimum by extending the reach of western crude oil via such projects as the Sarnia-to-Montreal Interprovincial Pipeline extension, and the emergency movement of oil to the East Coast via tankers from Puget Sound in 1974.

The situation in 1982 was different: there were no obvious short-run measures that could boost Canada's capacity to both produce and deliver crude to the Quebec and Atlantic markets. The precariousness of Canada's position was immeasurably greater than during the 1973 import embargo. It perhaps goes without saying that, in view of these circumstances, Canada should take every precaution to minimize the danger of large-scale disruptions to the flow of import supplies. The following recommendations have been made with this in mind.

Recommendation 1.   Canada Should Exercise Greater Import Source Control

Canada today has only limited control over import flows[82] and has yet to propound detailed import supply strategies (beyond declaring the intention to eliminate all imports eventually). International purchasing consists primarily of unregulated contracts between foreign-owned refineries and the marketing services of their parent corporations. The overwhelming vertical integration between the suppliers, the refineries and the ultimate purchasers has been the cause of concern in the past. As regards reducing the risk of future disruptions of both crude import levels and price, there are at least two areas that may warrant attention: first, ensuring some control over decisions with respect to where oil is purchased; second, taking whatever steps are necessary to guarantee the most favourable balance between contract and spot supplies as circumstances permit.

Some regulatory power over Canada's import supply system is essential to ensure both ongoing supplies of grades suitable to the refining capacity in place and the products needed by the domestic market. In this regard Canada should possess enough supply point flexibility that it can withstand the unanticipated and sudden loss of one or more sources, so long as the costs of such diversity are not unreasonably high. Canada should not continue to draw oil from one or two major producing nations and assume that a large cutback or embargo will be offset by the supply-sharing formula set out under the IEA Agreement. The IEA's demonstrated performance under stress is spotty, and its potential as a future means of maintaining market stability is doubtful. Should Canada be forced on the spot market to counter the loss of a major supplier, the costs would prove substantial in the extreme. For this reason the IEA's distress supply allocation system is less than fully consoling. Maintaining direct access to a range of secure sources under contractually stable conditions is an apparently superior option.

Supply point control offers a limited opportunity to hold import costs to the minimum. While OPEC's control over the international contract price is pre-eminent, from time to time there continue to be significant price discrepancies within its ranks. Once more, initial supply diversity offers at least some scope to take advantage of variations through selective purchasing.

Recommendation 2. Petroleum Import Compensation Should be Formally Tied to a "Best Efforts" Pricing Standard
Where possible Canada should limit the extent of its spot market exposure when spot prices substantially exceed contract prices. Canada's supply arrangements should be as secure as possible but with enough flexibility to avoid over-reliance upon any one source. In the

past, Canada's experience with the marketing services of the major international oil companies has been mixed in this regard. The unilateral Imperial Oil cutbacks of Venezuelan crude referred to earlier would have had a substantial effect on East Coast refining operations in the winter of 1978. After some tugging between the federal government, Imperial Oil's head office in Toronto, and Exxon's New York headquarters, the shortfall for Canadian refineries was reduced.[83] By contrast, Gulf Canada's refining operations were seriously affected by the 1978 loss of Iranian crude output, but Gulf voluntarily obtained the supplies needed for its Point Tupper runs from Kuwait. In short, the present worldwide marketing systems to which most of the major Canadian refineries are bound are capable of providing a large amount of security through supply flexibility.[84] Any problems Canada might have relate to both the locus and the profit preoccupations of the management of the international market networks. Without exception these companies report to corporate head offices based in foreign countries, the United States and Great Britain in particular. Profit maximization rather than cost minimization is the guiding principle behind the market decisions of such companies. While maintaining harmonious relations with consuming governments may temper the profit drive from time to time, the majors' market systems nonetheless are presently beyond Canada's legal power to regulate in the event of a clear stand-off between Canada's best interests and the profit opportunities available within the international marketplace.

Despite a brief trend in favour of state-to-state purchases, Canada ultimately will have to depend upon the multinationals for a large proportion of its import purchases over the foreseeable future. Therefore, it may be advisable to erect mechanisms to minimize the risk of a conflict between the profit objectives of the international suppliers and the effort to keep import costs as low as possible.

At present the integrated international marketing systems obscure an accurate determination of the precise source or cost of the oil destined for Canadian refineries. The possibility of less secure and more expensive spot oil being sold in one market to free up more contract oil for sale in another where there may be more favourable profit opportunities remains a concern. Government tracking of import costs is a necessary first step towards determining the extent of and preventing such abuse. At present the Import Compensation Program contains a limited safeguard designed to keep import supplies within an overall regional average cost. Under this scheme refineries are eligible to claim the difference between a computed average crude import cost

22

and the regulated domestic price.[85] But this system has limitations. First, it serves only as a check against a single refinery or small group of refiners attempting to dispose of disproportionately high percentages of more costly spot crude and make up the difference through the Import Compensation Fund. Second, while there is no doubt about the usefulness of the present system as a short-run restraint, it is deficient to the extent that it does nothing to moderate long-term average cost trends. More direct effort by government as a regulator, and possibly as an international purchaser, might be advisable. At the least, improved tracking to the source and precise monitoring of prices actually paid are advised as a means of both checking against actual abuse, and developing an accurate sense of the functioning of the international market.

As noted above, import source guidelines are a needed first step towards obtaining the security of supply that may come with greater source diversity. If these guidelines are adjusted periodically in response to market price differentials, and if the respective quantities of contract supplies are kept under review, there would appear to be some scope for the development of a cost data bank against which import charges might be held under closer supervision. It should, for example, be possible to determine the relative quantities of contract as opposed to spot oil that should be entering the country, as well as the fair average landed cost that Atlantic refineries should be paying for international oil.

Recommendation 3. A Petroleum Import Control Board Should be Created with the Discretionary Authority to Purchase in its Own Right
At present Canada is ill-prepared to assume complete control over its import supply purchases. Such a step would unnecessarily deny Canadian consumers the very real flexibility/security advantages potentially available under the privately-owned marketing services of the oil majors. But recent history has also demonstrated that the pre-eminent position enjoyed by these same enterprises will occasionally work to the disadvantage of Canadian consumers if they are not supervised to some extent. The value of having a system of controls at least available when needed would seem self-evident in this connection. It is thus recommended that a Petroleum Import Control Board be established.

Under normal circumstances the Petroleum Import Control Board (PICB) should assume the responsibility for monitoring source diversity and cost data, and establishing and enforcing source and cost guidelines. Where discrepancies develop between PICB cost standards and costs actually experienced, the board should hear and review evidence, and if necessary order compliance. To ensure that this jurisdiction is respected and that the PICB has adequate powers of enforcement, it is also recommended that it assume responsibility for administering the Petroleum Import Compensation Program and, if necessary, adjusting compensation outlays under the scheme to ensure adherence to import cost guidelines. It should also be clear that PICB price guidelines ought to reflect actual analysis of the conditions of the market, and not simply be based upon an average of refining feedstock costs computed from time to time.

It is not anticipated that, under normal circumstances, the PICB would assume the role of a purchasing agent for the refineries. But the board should be capable of assuming a more direct role with respect to security storage (see discussion under recommendation 4, below) and prepared to act as both agent and broker with respect to the acquisition and disposition of such supplies.

Under exceptional circumstances such as might result from a major supply interruption, the PICB should have the power to assume complete control over imports with respect to source and cost regulation, the use of storage facilities, and allocation between the refineries. Additionally, if PICB monitoring indicates a consistent pattern of unduly high pricing of imports, jurisdiction over all purchasing and refinery sales should be assumed by the board to hold costs down.

Recommendation 4. Import Crude Storage Capacity Should be Upgraded

Under the IEA Agreement, Canada is obligated to maintain sufficient import reserves to satisfy market needs for a three-month period. Reaching this target has, in view of the competitive nature of Canadian Atlantic refinery operations and high interest rates, proven to be difficult. However, there is indisputable value in at least the maintenance of reserve storage *capacity* sufficient to exceed the three-month IEA stipulations. More than just security of supply is at issue here. Reserve storage is a precondition to exploitation of price variations within the international market. When spot transactions play a larger role in the movement of international petroleum supplies, the ability to acquire reserves during price-depressed periods might ultimately prove a controlling factor over future Atlantic import costs.[86]

The PICB should comprehensively analyze Quebec and Atlantic storage facilities with an eye towards an initial doubling of the present capacity. The new storage facilities should be administered by the board and charges levied against refineries that in time will permit full-user financing. Moreover, the PICB should also retain the power to allocate stored crude supplies among the refiners should a decision be made deliberately to increase overall drawdown.

Federal Regulation of Energy 2

The National Energy Program (NEP), even as modified in 1982, represents a major accomplishment: it is Canada's first comprehensive attempt at controlling the broad outlines of future energy development since the "Great Pipeline Controversy" of the late 1950s. Through a broad array of controls and incentives, the NEP has refocused exploratory activity into the so-called "Canada Lands" frontiers and synthetic technologies and has (to some degree) de-emphasized "conventional" activities. The NEP has also reformulated and extended the mechanisms through which crude prices from various sources can be brought within a referencing (averaging) system. In short, the NEP has established clear development priorities for the country and implemented the rudiments of an oil and gas marketing system. What remains for consideration is the extension of these initiatives into the marketing sphere in order to buttress control over future development initiatives. Uncertain project economics, rapidly changing market conditions, and widespread uncertainties about the domestic policy framework have combined to make project advancement difficult, if not frequently impossible, in both frontier and synthetic production. The inevitable collapse of some of the major projects has frustrated the build-up of much-needed technical and industrial infrastructure to support future development. To secure its energy development targets, Canada may find it necessary to stabilize project economics and priorize new developments on a far more individualized basis than in the past. In this context, some of the initiatives of the NEP may have provided a useful entrée to a fuller range of controls under a national marketing plan. In particular, it will be argued that there is a need to regulate pricing of not only conventional gas and oil with synthetics and imports, but also a variety of other sources from various geographic locations.

The analysis that follows is divided into two parts. Chapter 2 outlines some of the major highlights of the National Energy Program. Chapter 3 considers the existing federal regulatory system, the role of the National Energy Board, and some structural obstacles that may inhibit the implementation of some of the NEP's major objectives.

The National Energy Program was unveiled on October 28, 1980 as a companion to the federal budget introduced during the same sitting. It represented a breathtaking departure from previous federal energy policies. That the NEP would succeed in generating substantial controversy was a foregone conclusion from the outset. Yet the debate up to mid 1982 failed to account for the full range of measures that the program in fact advances, and to this extent, the main features of the NEP are perhaps not fully understood.

The Supply Outlook

The most striking feature of the National Energy Program is the central position occupied by the so-called "off-oil policy" in the effort to achieve a long-term, sustainable balance between oil demand and supply. The specific objective here is to reduce residential, commercial and industrial oil consumption so that it accounts for not more than 10 per cent of total primary energy requirements by 1990. Where before federal policy statements contained bold assertions about Canada's ultimate potential to produce petroleum and natural gas in sufficient quantities to satisfy future demands by any estimate, the NEP adopts a realistic, if not on occasion dismal, assessment of Canada's near-term prospects.

> Production from established conventional oil reserves in Western Canada will decline substantially over the decade. New discoveries of western conventional oil are expected, but are unlikely to be of sufficient size to offset this decline.[1]

The program dismissed the much touted potential of the Athabasca tarsands with the flat assertion that:

> . . .it seems most unlikely that large-scale plans could be brought on stream rapidly enough to close the gap between demand projected under previous policies, and domestic supply, until the 1990s at least.[2]

And, so far as the frontier prospects are concerned, the NEP adopted a perhaps sensible measure of skepticism when it suggested that "it would be premature and unwise to count on the frontier to solve the oil supply problem."[3]

With regard to the overall question of supply, the NEP's planners

27

appeared determined to avoid the pitfalls associated with bullish optimism — the principal one being the necessity of regularly retooling policies to keep pace with the decline in supply prospects. Compared with earlier federal policy papers, the NEP displayed refreshing candour.

> . . .all too often over the past decade, expectations with respect to new oil supply have been dashed: major projects have been delayed, initial exploratory results have sometimes raised false hopes. It is never possible to forecast the exact path of supply development.[4]

In a startling departure from previous thinking, the NEP openly avoided future reliance upon oil-supply-based solutions, opting instead for higher user efficiency and large-scale energy source substitution, which in combination were aimed at resolving Canada's petroleum dilemma once and for all.

The "Soft Path" and the Multinationals

The specifics of the so-called "off-oil program" merit close scrutiny, particularly in view of the dramatic changes experienced since the NEP was first written. Specifically, the factors that persuaded the government to opt for this route should be measured against current conditions.

Conservationists have often contended that a barrel of oil saved through greater user efficiency is substantially less costly than discovering, producing and delivering an additional barrel of new oil to a Canadian consumer.[5] It is hard to dispute the economics of this proposition so long as the "saved" barrel is ultimately available to the Canadian market, given the value of oil to be rising in time. Assuming this case, full stock ought to be taken of the gains of enhanced conservation efforts which take several forms, including:

- increased security of supply — due to lowered rates of take from conventional sources of petroleum production;
- increased value extracted from each barrel consumed — due to higher productivity in primary energy applications;
- increased value attributable to remaining reserves — due to the net productivity increase in consumption;
- increased production cost stability — due to the extended conventional life index resulting from lowered rates of take, thus deferring the production cost hikes associated with frontier and synthetic developments.

Undoubtedly these factors might in part quicken the interest of any producing government in the soft energy option. But while important, these advantages are probably not the major accomplishments of an off-oil policy. More significant perhaps is the establishment of the first Canadian energy strategy that is largely independent of the major oil companies. In the past, these same companies, with a practical monopoly over exploration and development activity, enjoyed a power over the success or failure of federal supply projections that was perhaps unhealthy. Often, the government, in making its supply estimates, relied upon the best advice of the same firms which were so often quick to point to "inadequate policies" as the best explanation for their ultimate inaccuracy. The so-called "inadequate policies" have consistently included industry complaints about price and the federal-provincial split with respect to royalties and taxes. And, as the likelihood of a major domestic oil supply crisis has moved nearer, the influence of the industry in the policy sphere has at times threatened to expand in direct proportion with the problem's significance.

But the federal government has shown an unwillingness to accept this worsening balance of power. The first major signal of federal concern was the creation of Petro-Canada.[6] Its introduction bespoke the recognition of two clear realities. First, energy strategies that presumed the compliance of the foreign-owned major oil companies were probably doomed to fail. Second, the political cost of continued energy policy failures could be heavy and would rest primarily upon government not industry.

The new federal off-oil plan in this context is a second signal that probably has unmistakable importance for the majors. It is in effect a declaration that industry recommendations about measures to encourage future exploration and development may not occupy a central role in the future. Off-oil as the new priority offers at least an opportunity for government to evaluate dispassionately the appropriate emphasis to be given to the supply-based solutions in the context of an attempt to moderate the need for, and hence power of, the oil producers.

From this perspective, the NEP's major achievement is perhaps as much political as technical: namely, the isolation and partial reduction of the role of the most potent players in the development of policy. Were the off-oil plan not itself a significant move in this direction, the program's other proposals with respect to revenue sharing, oil and gas pricing, incentives, and Canadian equity have preordained a more complicated future for the foreign-dominated oil majors.

Import Requirements

The off-oil program is to be accomplished without a massive increase in Canadian dependence upon other fuels. If successful, the program would virtually eliminate oil imports by 1990, drastically reduce Canadian dependence upon the development of new domestic petroleum production, and mark a major transition in favour of the consumption of more plentiful fuels and/or renewable sources of energy. To call this ambitious would be a massive understatement.

Import requirements in 1980 were approximately 425,000 barrels a day gross,[7] or 25 per cent of Canada's petroleum needs net of U.S. export flows. The steady increase in import prices had pushed Canada's annual import bill dramatically upward to the point where it had become one of the more critical components of Canada's overall fiscal position in two respects. First, Canadian oil imports had a direct and obvious effect upon the balance of international payments. At the then price of $32.00 a barrel f.o.b. for most market crudes,[8] Canada's import needs resulted in a capital outflow of $13.6 million daily or close to $5 billion a year. This difficulty occurred during a time when projected Canadian energy investments were capable of absorbing every source of capital available. Given the low marginal propensity of most of the OPEC countries to import Canadian goods, very little argument could be made for continued import dependence, notwithstanding some degree of projected marginal cost disadvantage vis-à-vis domestic production alternatives.

The second fiscal item adversely influenced by increased import costs was the total cost of the Petroleum Import Compensation Scheme. Under this plan, Canadian taxpayers lowered the effective price of oil imports to match prices paid for western crude oil. In early 1981, Alberta crude delivered to an Ontario or Quebec consumer cost an average of $18 per barrel. The landed cost of imported crude for this same period, according to federal statistics, was about $38 per barrel.[9] Thus, the subsidy paid under the Petroleum Import Compensation Scheme was in excess of 50 per cent of total import costs, and represented a total dollar gap of almost seven times the effective difference between import and domestic costs that prevailed two years before. Should this situation have continued, domestic transfer payments to import-reliant provinces under the compensation program would have been in excess of $3 billion annually.

Ultimately, the view that Canada should reduce its import exposure was probably unassailable, provided (a) that indigenous oil consumption levels could be moderated without economic penalties significantly in excess of those associated with the strain on the balance of payments account, and (b) that ultimate domestic petroleum requirements were capable of being met from indigenous sources of production at a reasonable cost vis-à-vis import costs, taking into account the spread of economic benefits through the multiplier effect associated with the development and consumption of new sources of indigenous oil and gas.

The National Energy Program contended that a 10 per cent reduction in residential, commercial and industrial oil consumption would produce an immediate saving of 320,000 barrels of oil a day, or the equivalent output of about three tarsands plants.[10] But while it is conceptually interesting to consider the immediate consequences of a program that will take a decade to accomplish, the off-oil target of 10 per cent does not of itself guarantee an improved import position. This depends upon the rate of decline of conventional indigenous oil production over the forecast period, the rate at which the frontier and non-conventional sources are brought on-stream, and, more obviously, the overall pattern of petroleum demands in the future and the role of technology upon fuel substitution effects. None of these factors are static, and to this extent the off-oil target for the residential, commercial and industrial sectors may not have a proportionately even effect upon the reduction of petroleum import levels.

Conservation and Gas Substitution

To support the off-oil target, a comprehensive array of conversion (substitution) and conservation incentives aimed at households, industry and business, power utilities, etc. were contained in the NEP.[11] The prospective productivity of these measures is undetailed. Nor does the program provide any statistical or analytical support for the contention that conservation rather than fuel substitution will bear the major burden of the off-oil target.[12] The NEP assumes only marginal shifts in demand for substitute fuels and renewable resources.[13] Perhaps significantly, the NEP makes a particular point of mentioning that the major fuel alternative of natural gas should not be seen as a future low boiler fuel for the production of electricity.[14]

Conservation and judicious substitution are indisputably wise, but the sparse analytical support offered by the NEP suggested a conclusion different from that drawn in the document itself: namely, that fuel substitution, rather than renewable resources and conservation, would carry the major burden of the off-oil target (assuming it is in fact reached). For instance, between 1979 and 1990 it was assumed

31

that Canadian energy demands would expand by an equivalent of one million barrels a day (bl/d).[15] Over this same period, oil consumption was projected to drop by 416,700 bl/d. Substitute fuels plus renewable resources of course account for the full difference of 1,416,700 bl/d equivalent in 1990. But significantly, fuel substitution in the form of natural gas and coal amounts to 30.3 and 12.7 per cent respectively, or a total of 43 per cent, of the difference.[16] Electricity represents close to 40 per cent and, to the extent that coal or natural gas may be applied to electrical generation, the percentage significance of both fuels may well prove higher than the 43 per cent indicated.[17]

The actual contribution of the NEP's conservation measures between 1980 and 1990 becomes a rather difficult calculation. It is possible that in the government's mind the increase of one million bl/d equivalent energy over the next decade represented a major conservation accomplishment which, without conservation efforts, would be substantially higher. But if this is the case, it is an accomplishment that is the product of pre-NEP policies, for as early as November 1979, estimates by Energy, Mines and Resources of total primary energy demand for 1990 under policies favouring more intensive use of gas were identical with those presented under the National Energy Program: namely, 5.3 million bl/d.[18] The fact that the 1990 consumption figures are the same, despite the many conservation initiatives presented in the new policy, makes an accurate assessment of the anticipated productivity of these programs problematic. At the least, it is difficult to avoid the conclusion that, notwithstanding the contrary claims of the NEP, the off-oil targets will, if realized, be principally the result of fuel substitution (43%), more intensive domestic exploitation of electrical generating capacity (40%), and to a smaller degree, the contribution of renewable resources and liquid petroleum gases (LPGs).[19]

Refining Capacity

At present Canada lacks the refining capacity to make best use of all of its indigenous and available offshore crude slates. So far as domestic supplies are concerned, refining problems substantially limit Canada's short-term self-sufficiency to a level below what Canadian output on paper would otherwise indicate. To offset these difficulties, the NEP proposed extensive modifications to Canadian refining capacity. The core difficulty lay with the over-production of heavy fuel oil which, in 1980, totalled an estimated 155,000 bl/d.[20] With a combination of incentives, concessions and direct investments, federal planners hoped

32

to reduce heavy fuel output significantly and lessen competition between residual fuels, natural gas and wood waste fuel. Modifications now scheduled by Petrosar, Suncor, Imperial and Ultramar were projected to reduce output by some 75,000 bl/d.[21] Petro-Canada also examined a central upgrading facility in the Montreal market area, which could reduce production of residual fuels by a further 80,000 bl/d.[22]

Additional plans were offered by the NEP to improve Canadian capacity to make full use of indigenous heavy crude production. Heavy crude reserves as of mid 1982 were roughly twice the level of light reserves. But heavy oils are problematic both in the production and refining spheres. Accordingly, the NEP set forward generous incentives (in the form of tax and pricing concessions) to encourage more recovery enhancement investment. At the refining end, a new billion-dollar-plus heavy oil upgrader (in cooperation with Saskoil and other investors) was proposed.

As a result of these measures, the value of domestic heavy oil production to the Canadian market will increase, albeit at the expense of current heavy oil export flows which will be reduced. The consequent extension of domestic self-reliance through improved product quality was but a partial motive for the upgrading program. The second major accomplishment was to be the improved market position of natural gas through reduced competition from the heavy end of the refining spectrum. Refinery and product upgrading continues to be a necessary precondition to large-scale substitution that is in turn basic to the success of the off-oil target.

Natural Gas Supplies

The federal government declared that "a key premise" of the NEP "is that gas is plentiful in Canada relative to oil."[23] As noted above, the proposed changes in policy in favour of gas substitution will only involve "a modest increase in the demand for natural gas compared to previous policy."[24]

The reference to "previous policy" is somewhat vague. The "previous policy" at issue was the then quite recent favour given by the federal government to expanding the role of gas in meeting future Canadian energy needs. On this basis 1985 consumption was assessed at an annual rate of 2,318 Bcf (billion cubic feet)[25] or 116 Bcf above the most recent prior "current policy" estimates.[26] The differential between previous 1990 consumption expectations and the NEP's revised requirements was marginally wider, being some 323 Bcf per annum, or 152,575 bl/d equivalent.[27]

But these apparently moderate quantities are in fact not fully convincing of the viability of what the NEP is proposing. At root are two fundamental issues. On the one hand, the NEP offers a percentage that represents a desirable level of gas penetration in the Canadian energy market.[28] On the other hand, it also offers quantity projections expressed in volumes per annum. This raises a question of what the program is attempting to guarantee — the percentages or the volumes? It is a critical question, for should Canada's total energy requirements rise at a faster rate than anticipated, will the percentage role of natural gas be the target to follow, or will the estimated annual quantities be the guide instead? If the NEP is an attempt to establish dependable future percentages, there may be some doubts about the workability of the proposals.

The NEP's projected fuel shares, expressed as percentages, are set out in Table 2-1. However useful such a breakdown may be, percentages add little detail to feasibility. The basic reality appears to be that the proportional significance of natural gas will increase in the face of projected growth to Canada's absolute energy requirements. The NEP in this respect adopts an optimistic position about future natural gas prospects, contending that:

. . .even based on a conservative supply outlook, there will be

TABLE 2-1

PROJECTED FUEL SHARES IN TOTAL PRIMARY ENERGY DEMANDS UNDER THE NATIONAL ENERGY PROGRAM

	1979	*1990*
Oil	42.6	26.7
Gas	18.0	22.7
Liquid petroleum gases	0.6	1.7
Primary electricity	26.7	32.2
Coal	9.0	10.7
Renewables, additional to hydroelectricity[1]	3.1	6.0
	100.0	100.0
British thermal units $\times 10^{15}$	9.2	11.3

Note: [1]Exclusive of residential fuelwood and solar energy.

Source: *National Energy Program*, p. 100.

sufficient natural gas available to Canadians, even with a major substitution effort, for the foreseeable future.[29]

This view was presumably based in part on the 1979 National Energy Board analysis[30] which indicated a so-called "accumulated surplus" of nearly 6 Tcf (trillion cubic feet) by 1990, after deducting anticipated domestic requirements, fuel losses and currently licensed exports. But this estimate raises some doubts. First, how reliable are the NEB figures with respect to peak day deliverability security for Canadian markets over the forecast period? Since publication of the NEB analysis, production difficulties have cut into one of Canada's two prime deliverability sources, Kaybob South. Second, the NEB, as has been its invariable practice, failed to examine relative cost factors. Thus no consideration was given to the possibility that rising average production cost trends between 1979 and 1990 could impair the value of natural gas as a major fuel source for Canadians in comparison with available alternatives. In view of this analytical oversight, the degree to which the NEP's proposed gas pricing policies can be considered reliable will continue to be a large issue. Leaving all supply questions aside, there is some possibility that adverse field gas cost trends may erode the purported advantage of gas relative to oil that appears to have been taken as a given in the National Energy Program. Third, to what extent have western petrochemical ambitions been incorporated into the analysis of gas availability from the western provinces? The new energy policy is unambiguous in its insistence that all new petrochemical facilities should be premised on natural gas rather than petroleum feedstocks.[31] Little account appears to have been taken of provincial estimates of forward gas requirements. In the case of Alberta, the Alberta Energy Resources Conservation Board (AERCB) in 1978 calculated that, should ultimately recoverable Alberta gas reserves total 110 Tcf, the province would be unable to satisfy the gas demands of other provinces beyond 1985.[32] In short, the best judgments of the regulatory authorities evidence substantial disagreement as to gas supply prospects over the next five years. Less certainty over much longer periods into the future is, on the basis of past experience, inevitable. However, in view of the reliance upon increased natural gas use over the short term under the NEP, current differences of opinion about available supplies create some large risks of yet one more major energy policy failure.

The fact that there have been no significant conventional petroleum discoveries in the last decade and a half, despite widespread expectations to the contrary, establishes a need for caution in future

35

supply assumptions. Canada took too long to acknowledge the implications of limited conventional oil supply. Planners were more or less forced to turn to dependence upon conventional gas as the one remaining potential source of energy "sparage." But the acknowledgement of the importance of gas has been delayed to the point that there is some concern about the adequacy of supplies in terms of the longer-term objectives of the NEP. Canada depleted vast volumes of its natural gas stocks by exporting to the United States in the late 1960s and added substantial new export commitments to this same market in 1979.[33] It is possible that the margin of safety necessary to save the NEP has been also exported, should the AERCB supply outlook prove more accurate than the view of the National Energy Board.

As noted, the National Energy Program was somewhat ambiguous about the precise balance between energy conservation savings and the gas substitution levels necessary to make the off-oil policy work over the long term. When doubts about the future of natural gas supplies are overlaid, the core foundations of the NEP may be in some jeopardy. In this regard, there appears to be an important circular dependence between lessened imports through off-oil on the one hand, and the capacity to commit capital towards satisfying the longer-term supply needs of the country on the other. A failure of the off-oil program is, in this sense, a likely guarantee of the collapse of the entire program unless a major new and accessible source of petroleum or natural gas is discovered in Canada in the interim.

Finally, the NEP discussed Canada's energy needs over a relatively short period, perhaps in recognition of the fact that Canada's energy balance after 1990 is speculative to the point of being beyond reasonable assessment. Unfortunately a number of matters are clear. First, present indigenous conventional oil supplies will be of insubstantial, if not insignificant, assistance in meeting Canada's needs during this period. Second, by most accounts, production of natural gas from conventional sources will also be inadequate, and will dramatically fall as a percentage after 1990, assuming that interim gas requirements can be satisfied.

Fiscal Implications
As described later in this analysis, the upward spiral of oil prices since 1973 produced massive fiscal distortions between the federal and the provincial governments. Federal fiscal obligations under the Equalization Formula and the Petroleum Import Compensation Scheme dramatically increased during the seven years leading up to the NEP.

Equally, federal tax incentives in support of new exploration and development have also increased since 1973. However, while Ottawa's burdens grew, its source of revenue did not expand at the same rate. The traditional mainstay of federal revenue has been the province of Ontario, which, in part as a result of rising energy costs, in 1982 had one of the slowest growth rates in the country.[34] By contrast, the contributions towards general revenue made by the energy-producing provinces have been fractional as a result of their relatively small populations.[35] Moreover, the oil and gas industry, due to the generosity of the federal taxation incentives, has historically paid only a small amount of income tax at best, with many of the major firms paying none whatsoever.[36] In short, Ottawa since 1973 has had to shoulder an enormous increase in terms of its fiscal responsibilities without simultaneous access to compensatory revenue sources. It was therefore inevitable that the NEP would contain measures designed to increase Ottawa's share of the rapidly growing oil and gas revenues that themselves had been the major reason for the development of the fiscal imbalances in the first instance.

The approach taken by the NEP was multifaceted. A new Petroleum Compensation Charge (PCC) was levied to place more of the burden of the Oil Import Compensation upon oil consumers rather than taxpayers as a whole. The PCC had no role beyond reducing the burden upon general revenues. Whether or not it threw off net revenue in the future for the federal government depended upon, among other things, the direction of world oil prices and the consequent status of the import market regions' claims for compensation. While the NEP suggested a possibility of a net revenue balance in late 1982,[37] the main accomplishment of the PCC was aimed at more equitable distribution of the burdens of the costs of the compensation program, and not the generation of revenue for its own sake.

The NEP opened up a number of new revenue sources, the two major ones being the Natural Gas and Gas Liquids Tax and the Petroleum and Gas Revenue Tax. The first came into effect on November 1, 1980 and applied at a rate of 30 cents per mcf (thousand cubic feet) on all domestic gas sales (with export sales remaining exempt until February 1, 1981 through previous notice commitments made to the United States).[38] Subsequent increases of 15 cents per mcf were scheduled every six months until 1983. Over the period 1980-83 it was estimated that this revenue source would generate a total of $7.3 billion.[39]

The Petroleum and Gas Revenue Tax (PGRT) was to generate

roughly $5.2 billion in revenue over the 1980-83 period.[40] As of January 1, 1981 this tax applied directly against net oil and gas production revenue at an initial rate of 8 per cent. No deductions were to be allowed. As oil and gas prices rose each six months, the generally applied rate was to be subject to review and possible increase. Like the Natural Gas and Gas Liquids Tax, the PGRT was aimed at increasing Ottawa's percentage of oil and gas revenue in pace with its expanded fiscal liabilities. No effort was made to suggest that both taxes would do anything but reduce the scope for the provinces to increase their take from the industry in future. But the NEP made an effective case for the need to distribute resource revenues in a manner that ensured that present energy-related costs (e.g., import compensation and equalization) were offset, that reinvestment in new sources of supply was encouraged (e.g., via fiscal incentives, direct public sector investments, and so on), and that new conservation incentives were put into effect.

Both the Natural Gas and Gas Liquids Tax and the PGRT were the source of harsh debate. Alberta and British Columbia consistently opposed the imposition of a Natural Gas Export Tax. The NEP's response was to maintain that an "export tax" would not be levied, and then propose a tax which applied to both export and domestic consumers alike. A large part of the opposition to an export tax on natural gas was a response to the Petroleum Export Tax of 1973, which was seen by the producing provinces as confiscatory, notwithstanding the fact that it at one time provided the revenue base for the Petroleum Import Compensation Scheme. Had Ottawa then succumbed to the western objections, it would have been necessary either for Atlantic Canada and its already vulnerable economy to bear the full and potentially catastrophic brunt of the OPEC price hikes, and/or for Ontario and Quebec taxpayers to pay the bulk of a similar compensation scheme funded through general revenue. Had the debate in 1973-74 included a public discussion of the implications for Canada's taxpayers of abandoning the Petroleum Export Tax, it is doubtful that the tax would ever have grown to become the major source of controversy that it was. Similarly, acrimony surrounding the Natural Gas Tax may have been misplaced from the standpoint of most of the taxpaying public, who would otherwise have had to shoulder the full fiscal burden connected with the growth of provincial production revenues.

Since 1973 the proportional significance of the Petroleum Export Tax revenues has dropped, as have the oil exports themselves. For this reason the initial undertaking of the federal government to share one-half of all such revenues with the producing provinces was not seen as a major concession and failed to temper the reaction of the producing provinces as a group towards the NEP's other tax measures. In short, the Petroleum Export Tax as a revenue source has been more or less bled dry so far as conventional production is concerned. Whether new sources of oil can be brought on stream at costs that will support a restructured export levy in the future remains to be seen. On the basis of discovery and petroleum cost trends to date, a compensatory tax on imports would seem at this time to be an equally probable route towards maintaining a uniform national oil price in the future, assuming that uniformity remains an objective of any future Canadian energy policy.

Canada's fiscal treatment of the oil and gas industry has been generous to the point that the country has historically been one of the most hospitable investment climates in the world. Until 1980 it was possible for some U.S.-owned companies to obtain two dollars in tax deductions for every dollar spent on wells in excess of five million dollars.[41] These cases were the leading edge of a system that obliged the public to absorb the preponderance of the exploration and development costs undertaken in the main by foreign-owned companies. Perhaps relying on the obscuring complexity of the system, industry has consistently and publicly claimed that disappointing discovery trends reflect mainly upon the inadequacy of the federal incentive plans in place.

Canadians have not only paid for most of the exploratory and development expenses incurred over the past decade. Until quite recently Canada maintained a hopelessly outdated permit and lease regime applicable to Canada lands that was unprecedented for its generosity. Under this system it was possible for an operator to tie up large blocks of territory virtually for decades without an obligation to share the equity of a discovery (beyond modest royalties) with the very people that provided the bulk of the costs.

Canadian performance by world standards has been rather out of step. While countries such as Indonesia have insisted upon state production rights as high as 85 per cent,[42] Canada has been content to forgo state interests in favour of maximizing the level of incentive to the industry. As in the United States, Canadian policy-makers have assumed that a healthy and prosperous industry would automatically succeed in generating substantial economic gains, and that it was therefore unnecessary to insist upon public equity in the production phase. From the U.S. point of view, such a posture has not been unreasonable in view of the fact that most of the major producers are based in the United States.[43] Canada, by contrast, is a "host jurisdiction," and as in most of the oil and gas producing world, it is necessary to adopt deliberate legislative measures to ensure that a fair percentage of the benefits of producer status accrue to the domestic economy. Without such controls there is no basis for assuming that foreign-dominated subsidiaries will gratuitously advocate higher Canadian economic returns in preference to higher returns for their U.S. shareholders.

In this connection, the National Energy Program contained a number of measures that were tailored towards ensuring a more equitable division of the spoils. But, in total, the NEP's efforts represented only a beginning. The vast bulk of future frontier activity under the new incentive program continued to be funded primarily by the taxpayers, with only a modest return in the form of actual equity.[44]

But the NEP did set forth significant changes to the existing regime. It phased out one of the most controversial incentives, the depletion allowance, so far as it applied to conventional exploratory expenses. At one time a depletion allowance of 33⅓ per cent of an oil and gas company's taxable income was available as of right, regardless of whether that company was actively in search of more hydrocarbons, let alone bringing new discoveries into the marketplace. Historically, the depletion allowance was defended as being analogous to capital cost allowances. According to this theory, just as capital equipment wore out in time, so too did oil and gas reservoirs. The reservoir and its contents were theoretically treated as being no more than just another capital asset, albeit the most fundamental one. But, apart from the theoretical niceties involved in this concept, as it was applied, the system failed to discriminate between those firms actively involved in exploration and development and those basically concerned about drawing every last financial advantage offered under the tax system without further commitment of capital funds.

Canada introduced a system of earned depletion in 1974[45] and thereby fully answered the criticism that automatic allowances failed to encourage reinvestment. But the principal opposition to the system remained outstanding. In view of the enormous rents being earned by the industry, could any logic be found for reducing the collective taxation load of this sector so substantially?

The NEP took reform one step further by phasing down earned depletion in conventional in stages until 1984.[46] But on the other hand the NEP preserved "special" provisions for the maintenance of earned depletion with respect to a range of new source investments, including integrated oil sands projects, enhanced recovery projects, heavy crude upgraders, and exploration expenses on Canada lands. In view of the likelihood that future investment will increasingly concentrate in the direction of those sectors qualifying as exceptions, as a practical matter it is difficult to avoid the conclusion that the depletion allowance is alive and well, and that its termination in the conventional zones was aimed more at encouraging a shift of capital in favour of the Canada lands than an expression of disapproval in the concept itself. Indeed, the NEP expressly took into consideration even the highly controversial super-depletion incentive which expired on April 1, 1980, and which the government had promised to replace.[47]

There was an additional fundamental fiscal change offered by the NEP. The future incentive system was based upon direct payments as opposed to less publicly visible indirect contributions through the reduction of obligations under the tax system. Despite the altered format, according to the NEP:

> . . .the National Energy Program will, therefore, use new federal revenues from the oil and gas sector to provide generous direct incentives for oil and gas exploration and development. These will more than compensate, in many cases, for the reduction of earned depletion incentives.[48]

From the standpoint of encouraging Canadian investment, direct payments are more effective than the earlier depletion system. The latter generally favoured the larger integrated, and usually foreign-dominated majors which had substantial taxable income from southern production and marketing activity against which the earned depletion could be credited. Smaller Canadian-owned frontier explorers, in contrast, were unable to take full advantage of depletion credits, and were thus unable effectively to reduce frontier costs to the low levels that companies such as Dome, Shell, Gulf and Imperial were capable of attaining. In this regard, direct incentives are neutral, at least in principle. When the NEP incentive qualifications with respect to Canadian equity are added, the small Canadian explorer obtains an effective preferential edge over the integrated multinationals.

The NEP's incentive grants were directly tied to the level of Canadian equity in the exploring company. Table 2-2, taken directly from the 1980 NEP outline, demonstrates the system in operation. It presents a picture of highly favourable terms from the point of view of

TABLE 2-2
OIL AND GAS INCENTIVES UNDER THE NATIONAL ENERGY PROGRAM[1]

Year	Provincial Lands				Canada Lands			
	Depletion[2]	Incentive Payments			Depletion[2]	Incentive Payments		
Canadian Ownership Rates[3]		0-50%	50-75%	75%+		0-50%	50-75%	75%+
Exploration								
1981	33⅓	Nil	Nil	35	33⅓	25	35	80
1982	20	Nil	10	35	33⅓	25	45	80
1983	10	Nil	10	35	33⅓	25	45	80
1984	Nil	Nil	15	35	33⅓	25	50	80
Development								
1981	Nil	Nil	Nil	20	Nil	Nil	Nil	20
1982	Nil	Nil	10	20	Nil	Nil	10	20
1983	Nil	Nil	10	20	Nil	Nil	10	20
1984	Nil	Nil	10	20	Nil	Nil	10	20
Non-conventional and tertiary oil projects, and crude oil upgraders								
1981	33⅓	Nil	Nil	20	(not applicable)			
1982	33⅓	Nil	10	20	(not applicable)			
1983	33⅓	Nil	10	20	(not applicable)			
1984	33⅓	Nil	10	20	(not applicable)			

Notes: [1]As a percentage of allowable expenditures.

[2]Depletion will be earned on qualifying expenditures *net* of any incentive payments.

[3]Canadian-owned firms must also be Canadian controlled to be eligible for the larger incentive payments. Individual Canadians are eligible for the same payments as firms with a Canadian ownership rate of at least 75 per cent.

Source: *National Energy Program,* p. 40.

industry investors. But while the position of Canadian companies has improved, the system of incentives, considered in light of the NEP's maintenance of the earned depletion allowance for Canada lands, still condemns the Canadian taxpayer to underwriting the lion's share of the costs of any future frontier activity.

Initial industry reactions to these changes was negative in the extreme.[49] In view of the highly generous pre-budget system of incentives under the Income Tax Act, such a response was not altogether unexpected. But while the new regime of incentives may have been marginally less generous, the amount of tax assistance available to the industry continued to be very substantial. The major difference under the NEP was the imposition of Canadian equity qualifications which had to be met in order to claim any of the new incentive grants available. In this regard, the sharp industry reaction, of Canadian and U.S. firms alike, reflected concern that the Canadian equity provisions would provoke a devastating slump in industry activity.

Amidst the rhetoric on both sides over the Canadianization features of the NEP there lurks a single and all-important question: Are the costs of the incentives to the private sector worthwhile from the taxpayers' point of view, bearing in mind the returns?

The geophysical prospects of the Canadian frontier have not been sufficiently attractive to warrant unassisted investment. In the past, on the strength of Canada's "need to know," an enormously costly range of tax concessions was developed to artificially promote more exploratory activity. In the case of the Beaufort Sea operations, the public was actually paying some firms substantially more than the cost of the activity itself. Clearly, at this point the "need to know" was robbed of its underlying logic. A direct public underwriting of the costs through a Crown corporation would have been far more efficient. Simply streaming public funds to the enormous profit of private investors (in this case via a U.S. company) without any reasonable assurance of returns of any kind was a less than totally effective deployment of public funds.

If massive public fiscal support of exploration and development is to continue to be a dominant reality of future frontier activity, Canada at a minimum should receive a proportion of any resources discovered at taxpayer expense. The NEP's proposals in this context were perhaps modest. The policy's incentive program continued to tolerate significant foreign equity holdings. The public's direct share of discoveries has been limited to a 25 per cent Crown reserve. Reduced to basics, should private capital be capable of assuming only 20 per cent of the costs of an investment yielding a 75 per cent equity, the public might be better advised to underwrite the entire cost to obtain the totality of any return. While so sweeping an increase in the public's involvement in the industry would raise difficult ideological questions, the principle of maximizing investment returns on a "bottom line" would be better served.

Canada Lands Regulation

The NEP heralded the long-promised reorganization of the outdated regulatory regime governing exploration and development in northern and offshore frontier areas. This was carried forward with the introduction of Bill C-48, which established the new regime to be administered by the Canadian Oil and Gas Lands Administration (COGLA). Bill C-48 substantially corrected many of the weaknesses of the earlier system, but its jurisdictional scope continues to be a matter of some controversy. The province of Newfoundland particularly has held to the view that it alone has the jurisdiction to regulate the terms and conditions that will govern offshore exploration and production activity.

At various points, attempts at settling the offshore controversy have been made with differing degrees of success. Prime Minister Clark offered the Atlantic provinces full jurisdiction, but it appears that little thought was given to the implications of the gesture in terms of Canadian energy policy, and almost no consideration given to the constitutional niceties necessary for an effective transfer of jurisdiction to be actually accomplished. The dilemmas here were thorny. Assuming the federal government had initial jurisdiction, for example, would federal acquiescence to provincial legislative power as proposed by the then prime minister succeed in binding offshore operators, or would they continue to be free to challenge the jurisdictional validity of the relevant provincial legislation?[50]

More recently, the federal government offered the Atlantic provinces 100 per cent of "resource type" revenue from offshore oil and gas developments until such time as their per capita resource intakes reached the national average, at which point the provincial percentage would be liable to renegotiation.[51] But as of mid 1982 the federal offer of settlement had been taken up only by Nova Scotia. Until the jurisdictional issue has been finally resolved, it is unlikely that any of the present offshore operators will be prepared to commence production, for, without clarification, the applicable royalty and other provisions related to production would be legally problematic. Simultaneous compliance with both federal and provincial legislation would be prohibitively expensive (if indeed possible at all).

A second major uncertainty with respect to Canada lands has been the shape of the governing regulatory regime. The system had continued in force substantially unchanged since the early 1960s. At various times successive governments threatened to revamp the rules to bring them more closely in accord with modern practice, and various minor amendments were made. In this regard the NEP followed a well-established tradition when it promised a new regulatory regime. But unlike previous policy statements, the NEP was specific in its proposals, and major changes have now become law. Included was a requirement of 50 per cent Canadian equity as a precondition to obtaining producer status, a Crown reserve of 25 per cent applicable to all interests on Canada lands however acquired, a Progressive Incremental Royalty (PIR) system that cuts in when the operator receives in excess of a 25 per cent floor rate of return, plus other regulatory stipulations facilitating government review of the employment of Canadian goods and services,[52] through COGLA.

There can be no serious debate that an overhaul of the existing regime governing Canada lands has been overdue. But, equally, there is little doubt that making major changes to catch up with contemporary necessity can have a disruptive and potentially restraining influence upon the pace of investment. At issue is not the content of the rules as much as their consistent application, which is essential for effective investment analysis. In this regard, whether the NEP's amendments to the total fiscal package will stand the test of time would appear to be an open issue.

Conservation and New Technology
The NEP set forth an array of specifically-directed conservation and alternative energy initiatives. They will not be detailed here. The new policy generally recognizes the need for Canada to be in the mainstream of new technology research and development. Combined with the comprehensive conservation incentives and substitution targets of the program, Canada should continue to progress over the next decade towards less wasteful employment of petroleum.

While the NEP put some of the burden of the off-oil policy onto the new technologies, it refrained from relying upon any single one of them. In view of the tentative nature of rapidly developing technologies and the economics of the presently available alternatives, such an approach is praiseworthy. As a matter of policy, beyond developing an environment conducive to the commercial innovation of alternative forms of energy, all that was left to do was to hope that one or more might prove capable of living up to the often extravagant claims of their proponents.

On the consumer side, the NEP set up generous grants to assist household and factory natural gas and renewable resource conversions,

45

and vehicle fuel substitutions, and extended the home insulation programs.[53] Demonstration programs were proposed, as were broadened government R & D commitments, a Small Projects Fund,[54] Enertec Canada (a new subsidiary of Petro-Canada),[55] and a range of other support programs. On a grander scale, the NEP committed large sums in support of utility off-oil measures, new coal utilization technology, and additional industrial conservation measures.[56] Here again a wide net was cast, in the hope that some or all of these initiatives might take root.

The Natural Gas Bank

The NEP somewhat tersely described the formation of a Natural Gas Bank, which was to have an ultimate capitalization of some $400 million.[57] The concept of a natural gas banking system has at various times been discussed publicly, and on at least one occasion was employed to large advantage, albeit on a limited scale.[58]

The pressure for a gas bank derived mainly from the gas producers themselves. Lured into the field as a result of increased gas prices and the prospects of new export and domestic markets, the producers bitterly complained about the temporary gas "glut" and the failure of the regulated Canadian gas pricing structure to provide returns for domestic operators on a par with their U.S. counterparts.[59]

It is difficult to determine how extensive the plight of the producers as a group really is. Gas properties that are capable of development are of established commercial value and will provide substantial returns in time. Indeed the NEP commitment to higher gas prices guarantees that gas left in the ground is an asset of appreciating value. This of course does not solve the problem for a smaller producer short on cash flow, for whom a ready market is essential. Presumably, producers in this group would find a banking system to be of some assistance. But public aid clearly should be tendered when needed to support additional exploration, and then in limited amount. The bank should not operate to further benefit innumerable smaller companies whose main ambition is to sell out their interest to a larger producer on the strength of a single strike or promising property prospect, for, in such cases, public financial support will probably not result in more drilling activity.

There are also complex problems involved if the bank is actually to purchase gas properties. How should it assess the volumes being purchased when there is no production history? If money is not put up front in face of the substantial doubt that will inevitably exist about a property's value, how can the bank actually get money into the hands of those producers that need it most? And if, as often happens, a reserve proves disappointing once production has begun, who will bear the loss? If the bank is to assume all of the burden, its value as an institution for the (consuming) public will perhaps be marginal.

Even assuming a banking system can be structured to discriminate effectively between an explorer genuinely short on cash flow and the less creditable components of the producing industry, and putting aside for the moment uncertainties about reserves, it is then necessary to establish a policy of how much support ought to be directed to stimulate new conventional discoveries. On the basis of experience, an excess of supply in the short term invariably leads to mounting pressure in favour of exports, which, when approved, will lead to less conventional gas in future being available to Canadian consumers who are as a result forced to turn to higher cost, more distant and largely hypothetical supplies in the marginal conventional zones or in the frontier areas. Should the Natural Gas Bank at the end of the day only stimulate greater short-term "surpluses," its impact may ironically be counterproductive, with the export market ending up having more access to Canadian gas as a result of the bank's existence. In this sense the bank will result in less being held "on deposit" for Canadians rather than more.

A natural gas banking system must find justification in what it in fact provides for future consumers. In the past, debate about gas banking usually centred around the possibility of the NEB holding prime sources of conventional deliverability in reserve in order to:

● preserve the maximum potential for Canada economically to substitute gas in Canadian energy markets; and
● incidentally restrain the upward direction of production costs by means of ensuring a large base of inexpensive supplies.[60]

The Natural Gas Bank as proposed by the NEP is not directed towards either objective. Its raison d'être is to provide support for the industry and not, at least directly, the consumer. In view of the problems and uncertainties in its path, it may not prove worth pursuing.

Recommendations and Conclusions
The NEP is undoubtedly Canada's most innovative energy policy to date, but it labours under a number of shortcomings. The approach taken is too immediate, being focused primarily on achieving a balance over the next decade. The ability of Canada to manage its energy

resources over the longer term appears to be assumed. In this important respect the NEP shares a large flaw in common with its predecessors: an unwillingness to address possibly unfavourable supply trends over the long term. While effective management of Canada's near-term requirements is indisputably important, new sources of supply are also urgently required. Yet the lead time for substantial new capacity in most cases is in excess of a decade. For this reason, both private or public investors and government planners alike will be looking to more distant planning horizons than are considered by the program.

The NEP contains a number of initiatives whose productivity is uncertain. The Natural Gas Bank is one example. Many of the conservation proposals are equally uncertain, albeit for unavoidable reasons. But while this may be so, Canadians are nonetheless obliged under the NEP to rely upon policies whose usefulness in resolving the demand and supply balance is simply unknown, and at the same time ignore firm development opportunities which might have facilitated ascertainable objectives.

The future role of natural gas has also been given great play by the NEP. In view of conflict between federal and provincial supply projections, concern over supply deliverability in the long term, financial, logistical and economic barriers in face of eastern natural gas market penetration, and the draw of the export market on Canadian reserves, there are serious concerns about the viability of this approach.

While the NEP wisely demurs from accepting any single estimate of future oil production from frontier and non-conventional sources, it does clearly assume that new supplies will be available. And yet the flurry of program cancellations that immediately followed the NEP's introduction, which included the Alsands project of Shell Canada, would seem to have delayed access to new supplies as a result of the new policy. For this reason, the off-oil targets of the program have become all-important to the NEP's overall success. Yet, again, the NEP raises some doubts. For example, more natural gas and hydroelectric power substitution is central to the off-oil plan, as is conservation. But, so far as the former is concerned, how are the provinces going to be persuaded to free up domestic gas and power supplies over the long term if provincial requirements projections are at variance with Ottawa's? In the specific case of hydroelectric power, much of Canada's "surplus" capacity is bound under contract to the U.S. export market. To what degree does Ottawa intend to repatriate such supplies, and will the netback to the concerned provincial utilities be as high from interprovincial sales as it is presently from international sales? To what extent will the east-west grid have to be extended, who will fund it, and what efficiency implications are there from less north-south power exchanges? And finally, assuming a worst-case scenario where conventional oil production continues to decline, the conservation targets are not reached, and imports become, as is possible, in short supply, how much sparage is there with respect to either natural gas or hydroelectric power over the short term?

The NEP hypothesizes an improbable demand and supply balance in face of apparently complex and difficult circumstances. Moreover, it does not address perhaps the central problem of Canada's "energy crisis": the need to develop and implement an energy marketing plan through which development of high-cost sources of supply can be stabilized in face of increasingly difficult project economics. Quantity by itself is of little assistance if production costs are such as to place frontier oil or gas beyond the financial reach of the majority of potential users. On the other hand, where supplies can be produced at reasonable cost, the so-called "economic rent" is larger and the value of the resource itself greater to producers, consumers and/or taxpayers, or all three, depending upon how the rent is finally distributed. A deliberate effort to capture and stream a portion of this rent from lower-cost sources to support frontier projects through a marketing plan may prove necessary to fulfil Canada's development objectives.

The NEP, as noted, had much to say on the subject of pricing and revenue distribution among the producing industry, the producing provinces and the central government. It did not address the issue of production cost trends and appears to assume that the gulf between cost and price will continue to exist indefinitely. This may yet prove to have broad importance in terms of the viability of the NEP over the long term. The ability of the energy sector directly or indirectly to "self-finance" is completely dependent upon the existence and persistence of a healthy rent component. As of mid 1982 the conventional petroleum and gas reserves continued to offer substantial rent-generating potential. Should this not be captured and redirected towards replacement investment to offset the depletion presently being experienced, other capital sources will have to be relied upon. If the private market provides a portion of the needed funds, what will be the cost to other areas of private investment? If government is forced to be the largest source of funds, what will be the cost to social welfare programs? Canada's future energy needs are so great that the connection between new investment and the capacity to sustain the broader capability of the economy to continue to generate employment and wealth simply cannot be ignored. There is every possibility that the adjustment to an era of high-cost sources of energy supply will be difficult and that we will have to exploit every opportunity that exists to mitigate the adverse effects of the transition.

Recommendation 5.   An Energy Investment Screening Service Should be Established
By most accounts, energy investments over the next two decades will be immense if Canada's requirements are to be met. With estimates ranging between hundreds of billions to more than one trillion dollars over the next decade and a half, obtaining the necessary capital and simultaneously preserving control over the peaks and floors of the business cycle will be difficult. There is a danger that even a single investment of the scale of the Alaska Highway Natural Gas Pipeline will precipitate significant economic distortions, particularly in the traditional sources of capital borrowing. This will add to the subsequent cost of future energy-related investments, if indeed it does not delay or rule out one or two altogether. With this danger in mind, there appears to be a need to screen large borrowings to ensure that the most productive projects proceed first, that investment redundancies are kept to a minimum, and that capital financing takes place in a manner that will minimize the adverse effects upon the economy as a whole.

At present, the diversity of energy projects at various stages of development in Canada implies a need to determine investment priorities. The simultaneous development of the tarsands, the Cold Lake heavy oil deposits, the eastern High Arctic gas reserves, the western Mackenzie Delta, Beaufort Sea discoveries, the East Coast offshore, and the Alaska Natural Gas Pipeline would seem to preordain severe economic dislocations. Should even two or three of these projects proceed simultaneously, domestic markets would be incapable of immediate absorption of the new supplies, and Canada would again be forced into massive exports in the name of justifying the original investment in the facilities. In short, premature approval of such projects without systematic establishment of development priorities will unnecessarily risk overheating the economy, and increase Canada's total level of exports with all of the risks that that may involve.

It would be premature to describe here the most appropriate means through which large-scale appeals to the capital markets might best be brought under regulatory control, or indeed the precise scope of regulatory jurisdiction necessary to contend with the problem. Suffice it to say that direct regulatory control on the part of the federal government might encounter substantial opposition from the provinces and would be debatable on constitutional grounds. But, within the traditional limits of federal power in the securities field, it would appear that there is scope to develop a measure of central control over energy-related capital borrowings.

At a minimum, a screening process should be put in place under which a particular appeal to the capital markets can be given detailed examination having regard to its priority ranking relative to other large-scale energy projects on the horizon, the prevailing conditions of the capital markets, and the current counter-cyclical posture of the central government. Additional consideration should be given to a consultation agreement under which a measure of ongoing control over a particular issue can be obtained. Assuming that a schedule of investment priorities has been established (see recommendation 6 below), any of the following measures might be offered, individually or in combination, as a means of ensuring the voluntary participation by the industry in the federal regulatory scheme:

- government guarantees — whereby the government stands behind a portion or the totality of the debt where bonds are being issued;
- matching grants — in cases of more extreme difficulty the federal government might consider the introduction of a matching grant system on a ratio that will encourage a specific project to be financed through the federal screening program;
- government interest support — through which the effective yield on a particular debt instrument can be raised in order to broaden its market acceptance;
- agreed participation agreements — under which the federal government through a Crown corporation agrees to take up a percentage of a particular issue;
- investor incentives — either in the form of increased deductions or tax credits applicable to bond interest attributable to a schedule of bond issues that have been cleared through the federal screening process;
- corporate tax concessions — such as accelerated rates of depreciation offered to participating companies.

While it is anticipated that the above measures would be sufficient to obtain the desired degree of central control on a purely voluntary basis, the federal government can, should it deem necessary, appeal to limited powers of compulsion to ensure participation. For example, it could force compliance on the part of all federally-incorporated energy companies. Moreover, as considered briefly below, other federal regulatory controls over the interprovincial and international operations of Canadian energy companies could be restructured to effectively compel participation. Finally, the federal government might, through its declaratory power, obtain jurisdiction to insist upon participation by provincially-incorporated companies engaged in operations of a scale sufficient to warrant resort to this otherwise extreme solution.

While the ultimate array of controls that might be necessary is presently speculative, the need for central direction in the future is less so. The energy sector will be the largest single draw upon available capital in Canada for the foreseeable future. Unregulated, the effect of massive energy investments promises to reach every component of the economy in a potentially adverse manner. On the other hand, a careful pacing of such projects can materially enhance the overall gains and very possibly reduce the long-term costs and consequences otherwise associated.

Recommendation 6. The National Energy Board Should Assume Responsibility for the Regular Assessment of Project Priorities
At present the National Energy Board has theoretical jurisdiction to broadly determine Canadian energy investment priorities. Apart from concern about the past performance of the board, there continues to be a need for its supervisory powers over the energy sector, albeit perhaps under clearer statutory terms than those now in force. Regular priority and planning hearings, conducted with the purpose of assessing private investment priorities and potential capital obstacles, would be a useful beginning. The board might then be empowered to recommend priorities to cabinet, having in view development opportunities, market needs, and the avoidance of the difficulties considered under recommendation 5.

As matters now stand, the board does consider priority and finance problems in a limited fashion. Certification proceedings under section 44 of the National Energy Board Act typically include a financial phase, and longer-term supply options including new synthetic and frontier projects are usually the subject of consideration during the supply and requirements hearings frequently held by the board. However, the initiative so far as individual applications are concerned has been left largely to the private sector, the board not having assumed the role of formally determining whether a particular project is timely in a general sense. While such an approach was perhaps wise under conditions where great doubt existed with respect to future supply options, discrete priorities ought to be developed as soon as the commercial viability of any of the new sources appears to have been established. In this respect the board should be prepared to assume a more positive role in the pre-application stage, and should attempt to defer the premature preparation and submission of applications that do not fit within the board's schedule of priorities.

Where applications are to be heard by the board, the practice of including a financing phase as part of the certification process must be continued. But the board should insist upon detailed submissions with respect to financial feasibility and not, as in the past, accept highly tentative outlines of proposed project financing based more on a series of "ifs" than on hard data. If neither new markets nor backstop reserves are adequate to facilitate the development of an acceptable financing plan, it is perhaps not appropriate for the board to sanction an otherwise deficient application through the issuance of a certification conditional upon the subsequent filing of financing arrangements. The present burden of the NEB Act would appear to oblige the board to resolve all major issues inherent to an application in the name of ensuring service to the public interest. In the ordinary course of events the board should deny approval to an incomplete application as being outside of both the public interest and its present jurisdiction.

With an amendment to the board's powers, consideration could be given to conditioning all board certification recommendations on the applicant's compliance with the central financing screening mechanism described under recommendation 5. Such a step would effectively extend control over all international and interprovincial pipeline operators (i.e., all those presently under the NEB's jurisdiction), and ensure that one of the weaker links of the regulatory mechanism is brought under supervision. For this reason, under extreme and highly unusual conditions, such as might apply when the first major trunk connection is made to a developing frontier area, the board might be better prepared to approve a financing proposal in principle, and refer the outstanding details to the continuing control of the screening authority.

Recommendation 7.   The Alaska Highway Natural Gas Pipeline Project Should be Re-examined in Light of Changing Conditions and Priorities

Canada cannot afford to undertake large-scale commitments that do not contribute to its energy supply base, in light of the economic burdens that such projects create for later investments. The capacity of the proposed Alaska Highway Natural Gas Pipeline ultimately to carry Canadian western Arctic gas appeared in mid 1982 to be in as much doubt as it was when the project was first conceived. Costs had overrun to such an extent that the pipeline's viability was being severely questioned. If the mainline to Alaska is not constructed, it will be necessary both to reappraise the value of exploiting the western Arctic gas reserves first as opposed to competing sources of supply, and to re-examine alternative delivery systems best suited to the specific area, including the so-called "Y Line" advanced by Polar Gas and/or employment of ice-breaker LNG (liquid natural gas) tankers.

The decision of the NEB to recommend the dedication of additional conventional exports to the southern "pre-build" was widely explained as a useful means of easing the financing burdens involved in the entire Alaska Highway Project. Whether or not the pre-build would have received public acceptance as a "stand alone" export project unconnected to the overall undertaking is entirely conjectural. But should the main project prove to be no longer feasible, let alone useful from the Canadian point of view, the recent exports will not be re-evaluated or amended, as the NEB in fact did recommend approval on a "stand alone basis" despite the fact that the Alaska Highway Project's fortunes were improved by the decision.

Throughout the regulatory debate and international negotiations concerning the project, the value of Canadian provision of a land bridge for U.S. convenience has been eclipsed by Canada's apparent concern over the employment and industrial spin-offs connected with the pipeline. No serious effort has been made to evaluate the massive economic dislocations that may attend its construction, let alone the distinct likelihood that Canada would be better off were it not to proceed at all.

The Alaska Highway Pipeline is foremost an American project for U.S. benefit. Its value for Canada is far from clear. It involves no direct connection of Canadian gas to Canadian markets and offers no more than a possibility of a domestic conduit, assuming that an already costly and technically and environmentally problematic lateral becomes financially sound and can draw upon a large backstop of gas reserves, which as of mid 1982 remained hypothetical. If the

Americans have a need for the project, they alone should be prepared to take whatever steps are necessary to ensure its completion, including the necessary financial guarantees.

Other major energy projects better qualify as candidates for any special Canadian assistance, if for no other reason than the fact that most offer both energy as well as jobs for the Canadian economy. However, a withdrawal of the certificate of public convenience and necessity already issued to the project is not recommended. Mere insistence upon compliance with the original terms and conditions of the approvals, plus a firm statement of policy against the provision of guarantees, will reduce the chance of Canada once again massively subsidizing U.S. export markets to almost nil.

The Northern Pipeline Agency should in this event be either wound down or have its mandate broadened to include all northern transmission systems. Should this be the preferred course, consideration might be given to formally subordinating its functions to the National Energy Board. Not only would such a measure streamline a costly overlap and an unnecessary confusion of jurisdictions, it would also enhance the board's power to monitor compliance with the original terms of certification, and localize within the tribunal greater operational expertise in northern pipeline and other transmission systems.

Recommendation 8.   An Independent Task Force Should be Established to Assess Present Canadian Energy Supply Status
The NEP, like its predecessors, relied heavily upon the accuracy of Energy, Mines and Resources and National Energy Board assessments of Canada's energy supplies, particularly so far as petroleum and natural gas were concerned. As noted repeatedly above, the new policy critically depends upon the particular assumption that Canada's present stocks of natural gas represent sufficient deliverability to permit substantial reliance upon this fuel in existing and new Canadian markets in future. There continues to be doubt on this and other supply assumptions which should be quickly examined and put to rest (if possible). For the most part, the issue is a technical one: What quantities of remaining conventional oil and gas can this country reasonably expect to be able to produce and for how long? Equally, it is necessary to obtain quickly a detailed assessment of the amount of reserve hydroelectric capacity available, the domestic markets most able to employ it, and the cost and lead times involved in upgrading east-west grids.

So far as industry policy issues are concerned, a deliberate effort should be made to confine the scope of the inquiry to "here and now" issues. The NEP has advanced positions with respect to the most equitable basis upon which *future* exploration and development should take place, which have, with some modification, found their test in actual application. The task force should consider the hard issues of what is *presently* available and how to make more effective use of it, and assess the costs of various alternatives.

Not only should the scope of this inquiry be limited, so too should its tenure and its membership. It should report within a year, and its findings should be made public within 18 months. Its membership should emphasize directly relevant technical backgrounds in the energy industry. Should its findings prove materially lower than current NEB estimates, all pending (conventional) natural gas export applications should be heard on the assumed validity of the lower figures. No new gas export permits should be approved during the interim.

Federal Regulatory Controls   3

As the previous chapter has demonstrated, existing federal regulation in the energy field is complex and currently falls short of addressing the full dimension of Canada's energy dilemma. In one sense the present regulatory structure assumes, and may indeed have institutionalized, conflict between the federal government and the producing provinces, with each jurisdiction enacting legislation that may exceed what the constitution will support. To this degree the present situation continues to be highly uncertain.

The problems that Canadians confront are, however, less uncertain. Canada must have a stable base of energy production sufficient to satisfy the forward requirements of Canadian households and industry at reasonable prices. What is meant by "reasonable prices" are cost structures that do not force a decline in the welfare position of Canadians generally, or the comparative advantages presently enjoyed by major primary and secondary industries. As of mid 1982, available evidence suggested a likelihood of major supply and price difficulties in the future as Canada turned to high-cost frontier and unconventional sources for its oil and gas needs, and more sophisticated and expensive fuels for power generation, including nuclear power and coal. The sheer magnitude of human effort required to accomplish this transition, as well as the associated economic and social dislocations, suggests the need for strong central control. In this regard, it would seem probable that nothing less than comprehensive regulation of all phases from exploration to marketing will suffice.

Current legislative constraints influencing the development and sale of Canada's energy resource base broadly fit within two categories: fiscal and direct regulatory controls. Prior to 1980, the overall fiscal regime was the somewhat haphazard by-product of periodic amendments to the Income Tax Act. With the introduction of the NEP, Canada put in place a more finely-tuned system of fiscal controls that can, to some extent, respond to the particular needs of the energy sector. But the overall structure of the fiscal system continues to be complicated as a result of the interplay between measures aimed at the energy sector and the geographic distribution of tax liability, the claims under the present equalization formula, and the credits recently paid under the Petroleum Import Compensation Scheme. When all of these various components are taken into account, the determination of a "fair domestic price" for oil begins to assume a highly elusive quality.

This chapter describes the overall fiscal structure, and examines the main central federal regulatory agency, the National Energy Board. The purpose of this format is to demonstrate first, that energy supply and pricing decisions have an influence that inescapably involves the broad economic fabric of the country, and second, that Canada's energy sector continues to be under-regulated by a tribunal that continues to treat the subject as if it could be isolated as a topic distinct from the overall economic welfare of the nation.

The Fiscal Balance

As noted in chapter 2, the National Energy Program has introduced important measures aimed at expanding the federal government's share of the revenue generated by oil and gas production. The rents involved in conventional production are awesome, and even with the new federal taxes, the producing provinces still obtain a higher percentage than either industry or the federal government. The NEP estimated, for example, that Alberta would receive more than $100 billion in oil and gas revenues on a "surprise free" forecast.[1]

For most Canadians the debate about oil and gas is principally one involving the determination of a "fair" price. The province of Alberta starts from the view that the world price is the best reflection of the "value" of the resource. Having reached this position, it is then an easy step to the view that the best estimates of the province's contribution to Canada can be determined by deducting actual provincial revenues from total Alberta oil and gas revenues pegged to the world standard. And indeed, if one is inclined to accept this logic, the indirect contribution of Alberta would then on a per capita basis be in fact overwhelmingly high, far higher than the per capita liabilities of any other province.

At the other end of the scale is the argument occasionally heard from both federal and provincial spokesmen which contests the justice in adopting the world price as the best measure of the resource's value. According to this view, a fair price is one that allows a reasonable (competitive) rate of return beyond costs, having in view current interest rates and the profit performance in other extractive industries. Because Alberta is not a member of OPEC, it should not, according to this view, be entitled to employ "the bludgeoning economics of a cartel" in its relations with other Canadian provinces. Similarly, the Alberta contribution to Canada should only be regarded as the negative difference that might exist between the domestic price less costs plus a fair rate of return. Up until now this has never in fact been anything but a positive number, and for this reason the Alberta argument in favour of a higher oil price is fundamentally untenable according to this view.

Regardless of whichever viewpoint one adopts, it was apparent as of mid 1982 that Canada's implementation of a uniform domestic price for western and imported crude oil is the most fundamentally significant redistributive mechanism in place. It alone has prevented an uncontrolled burgeoning of regional economic inequality in Alberta's favour. Indeed, the resistance to a higher domestic oil price is as much the product of the outdated nature of present revenue-sharing mechanisms as it is of any other single factor.

The massive growth in western provincial resource revenues that has occurred to date has had a darker side that cannot be separated from the overall question of developing and implementing an effective energy plan. Each new dollar received by Alberta creates a corresponding liability for Ottawa taxpayers, principally those of Ontario and Quebec, under a variety of federally-funded programs and federal tax concessions. The costs of developing the oil and gas industry have in the past been borne by all Canadians both as investors and as taxpayers. This is still the case, as is the fact that the Canadian taxpayer's contribution towards other energy-related costs, including the cost of regulation and supervision, import compensation, government services, and government investment and participation through Petro-Canada, PanArctic, the Canada Development Corporation, etc., has dramatically expanded of late. In other words, while production may be localized to a single province or a small group of provinces, the associated costs, both private and public, direct and indirect, are nationwide.

Comprehensive energy planning requires at a minimum a recognition of the linkage between an effective fiscal strategy and the long-term demand and supply balance. A studious collection and the channelling of a portion of the resource rents into new investment may yet facilitate discovery and development of new sources of supply at a brisker pace than will obtain if the bulk of the revenues from production are left with the producing provinces and the industry. At the bottom line, the comparative efficiency of the prospective beneficiaries at recycling rent into new energy-producing infrastructure should be the major consideration in rent apportionment. And it is clear in this regard that a dollar of revenue in Ottawa's hands is far more effective than the same dollar being held by the Alberta Treasury or Imperial Oil.

Unfortunately, Ottawa's current fiscal stability is under grave stress as a result of the "energy crisis." Indeed, since 1973 rising energy costs have done violence to the overall fiscal balance of the country in ways that are both obvious and subtle. In this respect, the fiscal changes contained in the NEP are modest in terms of the extreme nature of the current fiscal pressures that derive from the energy sector, and are long overdue in terms of achieving a fair distribution of the fiscal burdens involved.

The effect of Canada's energy problems on the fiscal system has been given surprisingly little public attention. To appreciate the changes that have occurred since 1973 it is necessary briefly to examine the major fiscal programs individually. Three all-important ones have dramatically changed with rising energy prices. These are: the distortion and subsequent amendment of the federal equalization system; a vast uncontrolled growth of federal transfer payments under the Petroleum Import Compensation Program; and expanded subsidization of the industry through the federal income tax system.

Equalization
Rising energy prices have allowed enormous increases in resource revenues for the producing provinces. But this has unfortunately provoked large distortions in the equalization system. As of mid 1982, these were substantial to the point that Canada's capacity as a nation to maintain a comprehensive, federally-financed equalization system had been called into question. For the traditional "have not" provinces equalization continues to be one of the central advantages of federalism. But it is more than simply a progressive regional redistribution system. Equalization is the tangible accomplishment of an unprecedented national effort to establish a degree of public service uniformity for the entire population.

The funding mechnism that supports the system derives entirely from the federal tax base. Of the total sums paid out each fiscal year not one cent is directly collected from those provinces whose provincial revenues exceed the national average. Because general

60

revenue is the source for equalization funding, the preponderant contributors are those provinces that pay the highest proportion of annual federal income tax. In this regard, the largest historical and contemporary source continues to be the province of Ontario. In view of the substantial primary and secondary industrial development in Ontario, this is not unexpected. But current circumstances make this fact something of an irony. They also raise a number of contentious issues in equity from the standpoint of provincial taxpayers, as well as presenting a major challenge to the future of equalization as a practical cornerstone of confederation.

To appreciate the current equalization dilemma the major elements of the system's operation must be understood. Equalization has been aimed at roughly equilibrating the per capita value of provincially-received revenue in those provinces where the per capita revenue intakes are below the all-provincial average. To allow wide discrepancies to develop and grow would condemn the poorer provinces to perennially lower standards of public service in areas such as hospital care, education and welfare assistance programs. Such provinces would have only their domestic tax revenue to turn to, and, without cripplingly high, if not politically suicidal, rates of taxation, they would simply fall further and further behind. In its most recent form the equalization formula aimed at "equalizing" twenty-nine different revenue categories, covering the full range of provincial revenue sources from sales taxes to resource royalty intakes. Thus a fiscally-deficient province under this version of the scheme would be one whose revenue in a given category as a percentage of the total revenue in the same category received by all provinces together was less than its population as a percentage of the total Canadian population. For example, if a fiscally-deficient province had 10 per cent of the country's population but was able to generate only 5 per cent of the total (100%) raised under the Crown oil revenue categories by all of the provinces, it might be eligible to make a claim (depending upon its overall position with respect to the remaining equalization categories).

On the other hand, where a province enjoys fiscal surpluses, such as is the case of Alberta today in the six oil- and gas-related categories, there is no liability. "Have" provinces do not contribute to "have not" provinces under the equalization system. Therefore, Alberta, which in 1979-80, for example, received some $4 billion in revenues from the resource categories,[2] did not directly contribute towards the cost of the "have not" provinces whose claims under the formula rapidly expanded as a result of the jump in Alberta resource revenues. To obtain an accurate assessment of the distribution of funding liability, it is necessary to look no further than the percentage paid by each of the provinces under the federal income tax system. For 1979-80 this broke down as follows:[3]

Atlantic Canada	5.96%
Quebec	23.60%
Ontario	38.87%
Manitoba	3.60%
Saskatchewan	3.37%
Alberta	12.01%
British Columbia	12.79%

The enormous extent of the difficulties posed by energy sector revenues with respect to maintaining the equalization system can be best demonstrated by using the statistics for the 1978-79 fiscal period. During this year the producing provinces received some $4.75 billion from the oil and gas revenue categories.[4] Without specific revisions to reduce the extent of energy-related equalization claims, the impact upon federal fiscal balances would have proven catastrophic. Thus the 1977 Fiscal Arrangements Act[5] provided that the total of energy royalties eligible for equalization would be reduced by 50 per cent, and claims arising from the energy categories at no time would exceed one-third of the total equalization paid out over any given fiscal period. Thus in 1978-79 only $2.5 billion of the actual total of $4.75 billion was eligible for equalization.[6] Yet, despite these restraining measures, the total fiscal impact of growing provincial resource revenues continued to be disruptive. This could be illustrated by pointing out that the per capita impact of $2.5 billion spread over the entire population was in excess of a hundred dollars! The equalization entitlement from the resource revenue categories of the province of Quebec, as a result of its population of 6.3 million, exceeded $630 million.

Historically, some measure of the problem could be seen in the fact that in 1973 energy revenue represented only 14 per cent of total equalization entitlements; by 1980 this had risen to around 30 per cent. Ontario moved down from the pre-eminent position as a "have" province to technically qualifying as a "have not" province. In order to avoid an Ontario claim (which in the 1979-80 fiscal year would have amounted to more than $860 million so far as the energy revenue categories were concerned), only the traditional "have not" provinces were made eligible to claim under the formula.[7] But even with the exclusion of Ontario, overall entitlements under the equalization formula have risen roughly threefold in just under six years.

The distortions caused by energy and resource revenues imperil the root principle behind equalization. The recent changes cannot be discounted as merely anomalous. At issue is the commitment on the part of the country as a whole to smoothing out tangible material differences in the level of provincial public service capability. Resource revenues represent real growth in the standards of living experienced in the western part of the country. To exclude artificially these revenue categories for the purposes of computing equalization is no less than a fundamental retreat from the core redistributive principle built into the formula in the first instance.

As a practical matter, circumstances have demanded a revision in the manner by which the equalization system is funded. While this has been a growing source of concern since 1974, as an issue it should be firmly separated from the alleged need to adjust/reduce entitlements through an amendment of the formula. The principle of equalization remains sound, but funding is inadequate and involves an arguably inequitable distribution of the funding burden. In 1973, Alberta was still receiving payments under equalization.[8] By 1980, the growth in primarily Alberta resource revenues had pushed the redistributive burden and added in excess of $4 billion to the cost of the system, more than 62 per cent of which was borne principally by Ontario and Quebec taxpayers. Alberta taxpayers, by contrast, were liable only to the tune of roughly 12 per cent. In short, the two provinces that have been underwriting the bulk of the payment to the "have not" provinces are also the largest petroleum consumers, and to this extent are being the most adversely affected by the same energy price increases that have been adding to Alberta's wealth. Ontario and Quebec have additionally been "paying" in excess of five times the Alberta contribution towards the "cost" of the extremely generous federal tax subsidies for oil and gas exploration and development, a large proportion of which took place in Alberta. And, again putting aside all debate as to the appropriate price, the Ontario and Quebec contributions in favour of petroleum import compensation have been well ahead of that of Alberta's, as oil export tax revenues have begun to wind down with the declining exports.

In view of the geographical distribution of the burden of federal funding, federal government revenues should not entirely sustain equalization. The choice for the country and the resource-rich provinces in particular is comparatively straightforward: either equalization benefits from contributions made by the "have" provinces to augment existing federal revenues, or Canada will likely have to retreat from the root principle and reduce entitlements through a further diminution of the formula. The political significance of the amendments made to date appears to have been buried in the complexity of the system itself. For possibly this reason one of the most fundamental practical aspects of confederation has been amended with scarcely a public comment.

Petroleum Import Compensation
Canada's oil import compensation program has been administered by the Petroleum Compensation Board of the Department of Energy, Mines and Resources under the authority of the Petroleum Administration Act.[9] The board commenced operations in 1974, thereafter assuming responsibility for establishing compensation rates. Initially, compensation was paid to importers on a cargo-by-cargo basis, but this suffered from major shortcomings, principally in the form of not providing an incentive for importers to find the cheapest oil available. At one stage, in face of Venezuelan crude becoming relatively cheaper, importers began to switch in favour of the more costly and therefore heavily compensated Middle Eastern sources of supply. There was also some apprehension that even the less expensive Middle Eastern crudes from Saudi Arabia were also being diverted to other markets during this period.[10]

In response to these concerns the Petroleum Compensation Board attempted to fashion procedures that would provide an incentive for importers to search out low-cost supplies. The mechanism chosen was the use of a "flat-rate" or "average-cost" compensation basis under which an overall average for imports into the eastern region was calculated, including specific allowances for freight costs and quality differentials. In this fashion the scope that formerly existed under the cargo-by-cargo system to dump large volumes of spot crudes or exceptionally costly contract supplies was eliminated.

The compensation scheme has frequently been the source of controversy. At several points the Canadian subsidiaries of the multinationals have attempted to force upward adjustments in the rates. Gulf, in one notable incident, said it would not off-load a cargo of Saudi crude at Point Tupper until the compensation scheme was adjusted to cover alleged differences between the then current OPEC surcharged rates and the average price cost standard.[11] In face of the fact that no other importer was at that time prepared to make the identical complaint,[12] the government held its ground.

The compensation system as presently administered[13] undoubtedly offers a higher return to the importer with the greatest access to the cheaper crudes available under the multi-tier pricing practices of OPEC. For example, Saudi oil has consistently been available at posted prices that are well below the average price standard of the cartel, and the average price that is assumed for the purposes of compensation. There is therefore a substantial profit incentive for obtaining oil from the cheaper sources, given the present system.

There is, however, no doubt that the system itself has amounted to an extremely large and growing burden for the country. Some dimension of this can be seen by examining the growth of compensation pay per barrel over the past two years. In January 1979 the average rate of compensation was $3.00/bl., in June 1979 it had risen to $6.75/bl., and a year and a month later it had reached an astronomic $21.70/bl![14] At the 1980 import rate this meant an outflow of more than $9 million a day, or nearly $3.5 billion annually. Nor does this amount to a full statement of the problem, for, beyond the petroleum import compensation paid out, the government has assumed an additional qualified commitment to synthetic crude producers whereby their output would receive the "international price." This obligation was fulfilled by designating synthetic production as imported petroleum for the purposes of the Oil Import Compensation Program and compensating Canadian refiners who purchased it as if it were bought from offshore at the "world price."

So far as synthetic petroleum alone was concerned, funding was accomplished by means of a so-called "Syncrude Levy" or, more formally, the "Petroleum Administration Act Levy." The revenues that were collected were exclusively dedicated to payment of the international price for the output of the two operating Alberta tarsands plants through a Petroleum Compensation Revolving Fund. In 1980 this compensation represented a full 60 per cent of Syncrude and Suncor's revenues, and contributed to the payment of Alberta royalties as well as to the capital and operating costs of the plants themselves. Moreover, whenever the Revolving Fund went into deficit, the Consolidated Revenue Fund was charged by that amount, as was in fact the case for the year ended March 31, 1980,[15] when the deficit reached $75 million.

But the Revolving Fund was in actual fact the least onerous financial liability created under the overall compensation scheme. It was originally intended that compensation costs should be shouldered by the revenues collected under the Petroleum Export Tax. But as impending depletion forced down oil exports, the revenues available from this source naturally declined, while in the meantime rising import costs vastly increased the total fiscal burdens of import compensation. Thus the charges against general revenue grew to the point that this became the preponderate source of all compensation paid up to the introduction of the NEP. To this extent, therefore, the liability of the system fell in the same proportion on the various geographical regions of the country as does the burden of equalization. Ontario, in particular, again paid the lion's share, and unlike the next highest contributor, Quebec, received no substantial benefit (save to the degree that Ontario's refiners may have made use of synthetic feedstocks).

With the introduction of the National Energy Program came a reformulation of the funding basis for future compensation payments, but notably no major redistribution of the associated regional burdens seems to have been accomplished. Now the government will work within a blended price system, under which the costs of different sources of oil will be merged into a single weighted average price charged to Canadian consumers.[16] So far as imported oil is concerned, the new system will ultimately fold the total import costs into the weighted average price. This will be achieved through an extension of the refinery levies, with ultimately all of the refiners paying a new Petroleum Compensation Charge (including the Syncrude Levy), the resulting proceeds being devoted towards compensation of import-reliant refineries. By December 31, 1980 the PCC was set at $2.55 a barrel ($1.75 Syncrude Levy + $0.80 towards oil import compensation costs). Annual increases of $2.50 a barrel began on January 1, 1981 to be continued for two years so as to commit the refiners ultimately to the full cost of the program, and through them the country's oil consumers.

Briefly stated, the new system transfers the burden from general revenue (the taxpaying public as a whole) and places it upon the oil consumers who are geographically distributed on much the same pattern. Central Canada, with its industrial and population centres, will inescapably continue to underwrite the bulk of the costs of the new program, which represents in the main a mechanical improvement rather than a substantial redesign. A readjustment in the burdens will only result from a shift in consumption patterns that regionally alters the existing proportional distribution, which, as the drafters of the NEP clearly realized, would not come about quickly.

> Societies have strong "structural" rigidities: it is not easy to bring about rapid changes in energy use. Entrenched social and economic patterns, based on relatively cheap oil, must be modified but this takes time.[17]

The implications of this for the province of Ontario particularly, with again the highest percentage of the nation's oil consumers, are significant.

Income Tax Subsidies

While the oil and gas industry has been one of the strongest defenders of the philosophy of the private market and free (unregulated) enterprise as one of the most important forces of economic progress, it continues to be one of the great ironies of contemporary history that this same industry has been one of the most dependent upon government support in all forms, including the protection of markets, development of major transmission facilities, collection and provision of data, and ongoing subsidization of industry activity.

As noted briefly in the discussion of the fiscal changes set out by the NEP, on a worldwide basis of comparison, Canada's tax treatment of the industry has been one of the most generous. Canadian taxpayers, by picking up the bulk of the costs of the public sector in order to finance the tax concessions given to the industry, have "subsidized" the costs of most exploration and development expenditures, without obtaining any equity in the resulting commercial assets. The fact that throughout the history of the industry most of the equity was held south of the border made this state of affairs all the more in need of serious questioning.

While the burden of the changes introduced by the NEP is aimed at enhancing the position of Canadian equity within the industry, the amount of the subsidies represented by the new incentive grant program is still on a near par with the system that has now been displaced, so far as frontier and non-conventional investment is concerned.

Thus, in summary, the central fiscal reality of the current system is that, inescapably, the major burdens of equalization distortions, caused by the growth in resource revenues of producing provinces, the cost of import compensation, and the taxation subsidies and incentive grants paid to the private oil and gas industry, fall upon the taxpaying public, which is geographically concentrated in the provinces of Ontario and

Quebec. Ontario historically has not benefited from equalization. It also has been proportionately the hardest hit by the crude price increases of recent years, if only by reason of being the largest oil consumer, and continues to be the largest fiscal supporter of other government tax-dependent endeavours such as PanArctic and Petro-Canada, as well as all of the relevant government regulatory infrastructure, including the NEB, the Canada Development Corporation, the Petroleum Import Compensation Board, and others. At root there are major fiscal entanglements attached to the energy pricing issue that seriously undermine the apparent importance of the actual domestic price in force. No single price can truly reflect either the measure of financial benefit for the producing provinces, or the total fiscal liabilities for the country as a whole, both of which appear to be seriously understated.

Equally, none of these difficult complexities can be effectively mastered through a perpetuation of the present method of negotiating price settlements. Account must be taken of the full spectrum of fiscal gains and losses, and an effort made to apportion revenues in a manner that takes proper account of where the major fiscal burdens lie. At a minimum, this involves putting more emphasis upon the implications of any pricing agreement for the Canadian taxpayers, and less upon the symbolic value of the so-called "fair commodity price." Ultimately, energy prices perhaps ought to be regulated rather than negotiated, if for no other reason than to ensure that full account is given to the issues involved.

The National Energy Board

The NEP presumes a more comprehensive regulatory presence for the federal government than has been the case of previous energy strategies. But as of mid 1982 there was scant basis for optimism concerning the capacities of the existing regulatory machinery. The discussion that follows identifies some of the areas that may require structural modification in order to achieve a more sensible array of coordinated controls over Canada's energy supplies and their deployment. Of major interest in this context is the National Energy Board as the main federal regulatory tribunal with responsibility for energy matters generally.

The creation of the National Energy Board was the principal recommendation of the Borden Royal Commission[18] which had assumed charge of unravelling the political and financial chaos associated with the affairs of TransCanada Pipeline and Westcoast

Transmission's export sales. From this analysis it was evident that an ongoing regulatory presence was essential, at least so far as Canadian natural gas sales were concerned.

Following a format largely based on the Borden Commission recommendations, the National Energy Board Act became law in 1959.[19] Under this statute, the board today consists of nine members (a chairman, vice-chairman, and seven members at large) who are appointed by cabinet for seven years, subject to good behaviour.[20] Among other things, the statute expressly prohibits board members from holding any interest in the petroleum or natural gas industry.[21] The board is internally structured into a series of divisions, reflecting the categories of its responsibilities. These include administrative, economic, financial, engineering, legal, policy, operational research and environmental branches.

Following the Borden recommendations, the National Energy Board was given an enormous "public interest" jurisdiction. Under the provisions of section 11(b) of the NEB Act the regulators were charged with the:

> . . .full and exclusive jurisdiction to enquire into, hear and determine any matter and
>
> (b) where it appears to the Board that the circumstances may require the Board, *in the public interest, to make any order or give any direction, leave, sanction or approval that by law is authorized to make or give, or with respect to any matter, act or thing that by this Act or any such regulation, certificate, licence, permit, order or direction is prohibited, sanctioned or required to be done.* (Emphasis added.)

The broad scope of this section allows the board a wide power to act on its own initiative. In view of the extreme technical nature of the public interest questions at issue, and the additional fact that the board would be better equipped to identify areas requiring public intervention than would cabinet or any other arm or agency of government, such a broad grant of authority was clearly necessary.

To complement the wide mandate of section 11, section 24 confers the powers of commissioners under part I of the Inquiries Act upon board members. As a result, the board can compel both attendance and disclosure of witnesses, and is able expeditiously to examine, and refer where necessary, an issue for cabinet direction.

While the National Energy Board Act divides the jurisdictional responsibility of the board into eight specific areas, the discussion that follows has reduced board jurisdiction to three more general categories, namely, NEB advisory functions, specific industry controls, and controls over exports and imports. By way of caveat, it should, however, be noted that functionally isolating board responsibilities is slightly misleading to the extent that many of the individual duties carried out by the regulators are relevant to more than one jurisdictional category. For example, there is an overlap between the demand and supply analysis necessary in pursuit of cabinet advisory functions on the one hand, and the ultimate determination of an "exportable surplus" for the purposes of export regulation under part VI of the statute on the other. Similarly, the board's duty to ensure "just and reasonable" export pricing under part VI was in the past often critically relevant to its general obligation to promote the further development of domestic sources of energy (i.e., to the extent that export cash flows favourably affected exploratory and development investment trends).

Board Advisory Functions
For the purposes of fulfilling its advisory obligations, the board is bound to the provisions of section 22 of the NEB Act which, among other things, commands a continuous review be maintained concerning matters "over which the Parliament of Canada has jurisdiction" relating to: (1) exploration, (2) production, (3) recovery, (4) manufacture, (5) processing, (6) transmission, (7) transportation, (8) distribution, (9) sale, (10) purchase, (11) exchange and (12) disposal of energy and sources of energy within and outside of Canada.

Where the information obtained under this review suggests issues of public concern that require government action, the board is duty bound to refer the question to the minister of energy, mines and resources with its recommendations. Section 22 ostensibly relates to part II of the statute, but it is in actual fact a main cornerstone provision insofar as it requires that the board maintain an up-to-date command of the long-term implications of all types of energy resource development throughout the country. The enormous breadth of this duty lends some justification to the wide power that the regulators have to tailor their procedures and methods of investigation and inquiry as they go along. In this regard, section 14 permits the board to inquire, hear and determine any matter within the scope of section 22, and the act at large, of its own volition. It also has the power to delegate hearing functions to individual board members to ensure the effective deployment of otherwise scarce personnel. Finally, the board under section 45 has a measure of affirmative power over its duty to hear by virtue of having the purportedly conclusive authority to determine whether a person is an "interested party" for the purposes of the application of part IV of the act.

The board in some respects has an impossibly broad mandate. This has made wide powers of internal procedural discretion arguably essential. But at the same time there are large risks that are associated with this fact. First is the possibility that the regulators may be tempted to misuse their procedural power to prejudice a full and open hearing of all the relevant issues in a particular case.[22] A second danger is the possibility that an individual applicant or intervenor might attempt to take advantage of the initial procedural flexibility. As one author noted in this context:

> The Board, being an administrative agency, has provided in Rule III of the NEB Procedural Rules that it may direct that the rules or any of them shall not apply in any specific hearing or that it may substitute other rules for the established rules. This obviously has left the Board with a great deal of flexibility in the matter of determining practice and procedure before it. However, the provision for such flexibility has left the system open to abuse by applicants and interveners appearing before the Board in furtherance of their own self-interest.
>
> As lawyers trained to seek uniformity and certainty in the administration of the law and taught that justice must [not only] be done but must be seen and seem to be done, we share the concern that has been expressed over the uncertainty and lack of uniformity that is apparent, from time to time, in the practice and procedures of administrative agencies, including the NEB.[23]

It is a fact that unrepresented interests at issue in a given decision are often greater in number and in economic importance than the total interest of direct participants. Because this is so, both the public at large and the federal cabinet are heavily reliant upon the adequacy of the board's decisions and recommendations. Indeed, in this regard the term "advisory functions" is something of a misnomer, given the technical sophistication of the issues under the NEB's control and the historically-demonstrated inability of cabinet to manage the detail involved in such matters.

In one sense the board has had "educational functions" as well. Through its creation, cabinet was freed of the time-consuming intricacies of energy-related problems. But the price of this step was an unavoidable danger of receiving inadequate advice based upon data and analysis that only those giving the advice might fully comprehend. As a result of this fact the regulators enjoyed an independence that arose not from the terms of the National Energy Board Act per se, but instead from their superior command of an oftentimes prohibitively complicated field of jurisdiction.

The board has additional statutory duties of an advisory nature. Under part VI of the NEB Act the board must submit a report concerning export applications with appropriate recommendations in the event that they are to be approved. This report and the recommendations are advisory in nature, and the cabinet has the jurisdiction to accept or reject either at will. In this regard, however, the board has an independent power to refuse an application, in which case no reference to the higher authority of cabinet is made.

The board also has the duty to advise with respect to potential areas of cooperation between Canada and the United States concerning energy matters generally. The relevant provision of the NEB Act here is section 22(2):

> The Board shall, at the request of the Minister, prepare studies and reports on any matters relating to energy or sources of energy, and shall recommend to the Minister the making of such arrangements as is considered desirable for co-operation with governmental or other agencies in or outside Canada in respect of matters relating to energy and sources of energy.

There is no public detail concerning board activity under this provision. Such board reports as may exist are not public documents. There is, however, no serious doubt that the provision is of operational significance, and that board consultation has in the past been both sought and received by the government on such issues.

Strong impetus for higher international cooperation can be found from historical differences in view between the NEB and what was the Federal Power Commission concerning prices to be paid for West Coast natural gas exports. More recently, the desire of the United States to have advance notice of intended price changes has resulted in the creation of a three-month notice period. And the joint approval by the National Energy Board and the Federal Energy Regulatory Commission of the Alaska Highway Natural Gas Pipeline has necessitated ongoing joint consultation between the two government agencies.

Specific Industry Controls
The National Energy Board has jurisdiction over a range of specific areas of industry concern. All pipeline development, for example, falls

under its jurisdiction. A pipeline is defined, for the purposes of the statute, as:

> . . .a line for the transmission of gas or oil connecting a province with any other or others of the provinces, or extending beyond the limits of a province, and includes all branches, extensions, tanks, reservoirs, storage facilities, pumps, racks, compressors, loading facilities, interstation systems of communication by telephone, telegraph or radio, and real and personal property and works connected therewith.[24]

The certification procedures of the board centre around section 44 of the NEB Act. It provides as follows:

> The Board may, subject to the approval of the Governor-in-Council, issue a certificate in respect of a pipeline or an international power line if the Board is satisfied that the line is and will be required by the present and future public convenience and necessity, and, in considering an application for a certificate, the Board shall take into account all such matters as to it appear to be relevant, and without limiting the generality of the foregoing, the Board may have regard to the following:
> a.   the availability of oil or gas to the pipeline, or power to the international power line, as the case may be;
> b.   the existence of markets, actual or potential;
> c.   the economic feasibility of the pipeline or international power line;
> d.   the financial responsibility and financial structure of the applicant, the methods of financing the line and the extent to which Canadians will have an opportunity of participating in the financing, engineering and construction of the line; and
> e.   *any public interest in the Board's opinion that may be affected by the granting or the refusing of the application.* (Emphasis added.)

An applicant not only has to conform with this general section, but also must adhere to the regulations that extensively detail the content expected of formal submissions. In addition, the board has the power to condition any certificates that it might issue with such terms as it considers desirable with respect to the overall purposes of the act.[25] Finally, as is the case with board export decisions, a favourable determination in respect of certification must again have the ultimate approval of the Governor-in-Council to be effective.[26]

The board has an ongoing jurisdiction with respect to many operational aspects of pipelines. Most important is its jurisdiction with respect to traffic, tolls and tariffs under section 52 of the NEB Act. This section provides as follows:

> all tolls shall be just and reasonable, and shall always, under

73

substantially similar circumstances and conditions with respect to all traffic of the same description carried over the same route, be charged equally to all persons at the same rate.

The board's jurisdiction under section 52 is final. Moreover, the NEB has the power to act in those cases where it finds discrimination with respect to tolls, services or facilities that might adversely affect any consumer or group of consumers. The act explicitly commands in this regard that: "a company shall not make any unjust discrimination in tolls, services or facilities against any person or locality."[27]

Under section 58(3), the board has authority to intervene in industry price negotiations and, where necessary "prescribe the terms and conditions under which hydrocarbons may be transmitted by the company." Sections 53 and 54 complement this authority by allowing the board to eliminate or suspend a tariff or portion of a tariff with which it has taken issue. Sections 59(2) and 60 arm the board with the affirmative power to force companies operating either oil or gas transmission facilities to upgrade and extend or improve their services so as to increase the total Canadian market that is being served.

As is the case of so much of the statute, the board's jurisdiction over the operation of pipeline companies is a sweeping one. Its wide regulatory discretion in part derives from the imprecision of phrases such as "just and reasonable" (section 55), and the references to the "public interest" and "undue burden" of sections 59 and 60. On the other hand, greater clarity in the statute would be inconsistent with the advantages of allowing the regulators broad powers to interfere in industry affairs in the name of protecting consumers.

Export Regulation

Scope of Jurisdiction
In its export determinations, the board is bound to the provisions of part VI of the NEB Act. Throughout most of the NEB's history, this part has applied to natural gas exports, although its scope was extended through cabinet proclamation to include petroleum as well. However, oil exports are rapidly being phased out. As of mid 1982 detailed criteria applied to trans-border gas sales exclusively. Accordingly, these will be the main focus of the discussion that follows.

Part VI starts with a prohibition against unauthorized gas, oil or power exports.[28] The jurisdiction of the board with respect to the issuance of licences is set out under section 82. Of notice here particularly is sub-paragraph (3) which provides:

Every licence is subject to the condition that the provisions of this Act

74

and the regulations in force at the date of issue thereof and *as subsequently enacted*, made or amended, as well as every order made under the authority of this Act, will be complied with. (Emphasis added.)

Section 82(3) must be read in conjunction with section 17 of the statute whose intent is similar, and whose effect is complementary in respect of its practical consequences:

(1) Subject to subsection (2), the Board may review, rescind, change, alter or vary any order or decision made by it, or may rehear any application before deciding it.

(2) The Board may change, alter or vary a certificate or licence issued by it but no such change, alteration or variation is effective until approved by the Governor-in-Council.

Read together, the two provisions appear to give the board the jurisdiction to rescind, alter or otherwise vary licences after the fact of their issuances in response of the dictates of the circumstances. Procedurally such an action would commence through a board order made under Section 82(3). This would in turn be subject to cabinet approval pursuant to section 17(2). The Governor-in-Council, on the other hand, might proceed directly via new regulations passed under section 89, whose *ex post facto* validity is ensured by virtue of section 82(3). The opening phrasing of this provision would appear more or less to rule out any argument based upon a so-called "vested right" of a licensee. Even should the improbable argument succeed that a licence to export involves the conferment of a legal right in the nature of a contract (rather than being purely discretionary and at the will of the board and cabinet), the right itself has been made expressly conditional upon the other provisions of the act (in particular section 17 and the regulations passed pursuant to section 82[3]).

Beyond the discretionary rescissions and variations that might take place, export licences are subject to specific revocation or suspension under the terms of section 84 which provides:

(1) Subject to subsection (2) and the Regulations, the Board may by order, with the approval of the Governor-in-Council revoke or suspend a licence if any term or condition thereof has not been complied with or has been violated.

(2) No order shall be made under subsection (1) unless notice of the alleged non-compliance or violation has been given to the holder of the licence and the Board has afforded him an opportunity of being heard.

This provision contains the teeth behind the operation of section 82(3).

75

It would come into play the moment a licence holder chose to ignore an after-the-fact variation that was carried into play through either an approved board order or a cabinet regulation.

In short, the board has wide powers in respect of both the initial granting of, and the subsequent variation or rescission of, oil, gas and power exports.

Export Criteria: General
The board's duties under section 83 of the NEB Act have been its most active area of jurisdiction since 1959. This section reads as follows:

> Upon application for a licence the Board shall have regard to all considerations that appear to it to be relevant and, *without limiting the generality of the foregoing*, the Board shall satisfy itself that
> (a) the quantity of gas or power to be exported does not exceed the surplus remaining after due allowance has been made for the reasonably foreseeable requirements for use in Canada having regard, in the case of an application to export gas, to the trends in the discovery of gas in Canada; and
> (b) the price to be charged by an applicant for gas or power exported by him is just and reasonable in relation to the public interest. (Emphasis added.)

Once more, section 83 is a provision that is extremely broad in scope, and very possibly more significant for the many uncertainties it introduces than it is for those it purports to resolve. In view of the complex history that antedated the board's creation, and the technical sophistication involved in obtaining a working definition of such terms as "reasonably foreseeable domestic requirements," "discovery trends," "foreseeable surpluses," and "just and reasonable prices," a more exact provision would have been at best premature in the context of 1959, and at worst self-defeating in terms of the objective of giving the necessary leeway to the regulators to develop effective procedures.

It is, however, important to point out two contrary risks in this context. First, from the beginning it was apparent that the nature and importance of the discretion that this general section conferred upon the board was vast, and thus should have been subjected to regular scrutiny. And second, as regulatory procedures began to evolve, greater statutory clarity might have become possible, and appropriate amendments could have been added to temper the excess of regulatory discretion otherwise inherent to this provision.

Export Criteria: Working Procedures
Reduced to its most basic, the board's main function in respect of

export licensing involves obtaining a balance between demand and supply that can be maintained for the longest possible period of time. Unfortunately, so basic a statement of regulatory objectives involves ignoring complexities which have, since the board's creation, proven pre-emptive. First, the equilibrium sought relates to future conditions, and to achieve it, reasonably accurate projections of the absolute magnitude of both future domestic demand and future conventional supplies are essential. Second, obtaining a stable equilibrium price over time requires highly detailed information concerning a nearly impossible array of relative economic factors that can influence future demand and supply trends, many of which lie beyond confident prediction. In view of this, simply to maintain that the board has failed to achieve an "elegant answer" to the export dilemma is perhaps meaningless. The more substantial issues to be tested are threefold:

- Has the board fallen so short of fulfilling its statutory obligations to protect the domestic market that a generalization can be made about its overall effectiveness?
- What procedures are in place to mitigate the avoidable domestic risks entailed in export market service?
- Overall what should now be done with respect to the regulation of existing and future exports in view of a possibly changing complexion in the national interest?

An unfortunate analytical difficulty should be noted at this point. Any attempt at summarizing board procedures with respect to demand and supply analysis (on the basis of the record on hand) is rendered rather tenuous by virtue of the fact that the methods employed by the board have not always been fully explained in a number of critical respects (including notably the data-base sources to calculate reserves and requirements, and the working definitions of many of the terms of art employed by the board). To this degree, therefore, board processes have laboured under an occasional, often critical, and completely unnecessary uncertainty which has obscured a full picture of the history of the board's work.

As already noted, pursuant to section 83 of the NEB Act, exports will only be licensed upon the determination of the existence of a surplus vis-à-vis reasonably foreseeable domestic requirements, and upon the further proof that the prices to be charged in the export market are "just and reasonable in relation to the public interest." The board, in considering the merits of an individual application, must therefore dispose of four constant categories of uncertainty: namely, the value of

(1) the supply estimation techniques; (2) the demand estimation techniques; (3) (historically) the just and reasonable pricing test; and (4) the domestic requirement protection formula.

The problems that are involved in each of the above areas are protracted. The concepts of "needs," "reserves" and "exportable surpluses" are all time-referential rather than absolute. None need factually exist at the moment of calculation for they are mere estimates or probabilities based upon (a) limited data from which future trends might be inferred, and (b) a series of assumptions developed from prior experience. Because this is the case, errors can be (and frequently are) made.[29]

This potential for error is tied critically to the adequacy of the underlying technical procedures that the board employs in each of the categories. As noted above, the Borden Commission, with this very problem in mind, was at pains to stress the need for continuous review and revision of the regulatory procedures in force to take advantage of the most up-to-date and accurate demand and supply estimation techniques available. Unfortunately, a review of the calculus employed by the board reveals rigidity, deceptive precision and, in some areas, apparently unnecessary sophistication.

On the supply estimation side, there is definitional confusion in board discussion of reserves. There are, for example, references to "established," "proven," "proved," "marketable," "estimated," "probable," "potential," "possible" and "ultimate" reserves, in addition to "reserves beyond economic reach" and "deferred reserves." The terms are often left undefined, and where this is so, the underlying methodology that is being employed is obscured. Furthermore, in some cases the regulators and the industry have different working definitions for the same terms, which adds to the initial uncertainty. To illustrate, the Canadian Petroleum Association and the National Energy Board each have a separate usage for the term "probable reserves" and, in consequence, arrive at sharply contrasting figures. Finally, the terms are themselves misleading. "Established reserves" are usually quoted by the press, and sometimes by the industry, as if they represented presently known and certain volumes of natural gas and petroleum. The fact that, as a term of art, "established" includes conjectural volumes is frequently ignored. This same criticism applies to "proved" or "proven" reserves which are also contingent estimates based upon a *ceteris paribus* assumption respecting economic and operating conditions.

But even where there is a consensus as to the definitional application of a particular definition, the estimates produced often reflect sizeable variations which are difficult to explain.[30] In view of these discrepancies, it is clear that wide differences of opinion exist as to the underlying assumptions upon which the employment of the definitions themselves depend.

There is also uncertainty with respect to the source of reserve data used by the board. It is known that some information is drawn from provincial agencies such as the Alberta Energy Resources Conservation Board, from federal departments and branches such as the Geological Survey of Canada, and to some extent from internal board research. But, in the main, the industry continues to be the largest source of reserve information, and most particularly, the Canadian Petroleum Association. In view of the costs of developing a wholly independent data base, the reliance upon the private sector, and all the risks that are involved with it, is inescapable. It is thus of interest to know something of the extent to which the board is capable of "looking behind" the estimates, and the procedures (if any) that are in fact applied to discount industry estimates. For the purposes of estimating the total quantity of natural gas available, the board computes the so-called "current" reserves. The current (or established) reserves include both proven reserves plus one-half of the prevailing estimate of "probable" reserves. From this total a number of deductions are then made, including reserves deferred for the purposes of field conservation, and a portion of the reserves currently known to be "beyond economic reach."

Established reserves by definition involve the inclusion of purely hypothetical natural gas volumes in the board's current inventories. Because of this, the board has been considerably more generous in its assessment than is indeed the industry itself. As a matter of practice, industry and its outside capital suppliers demand sufficient volumes of gas in support of any new facility or facility expansion to ensure its viability over its entire amortized life. As an historical matter, however, the regulators' estimates have accurately described conventional supply status, and for this reason alone only a weak case can be made for the adoption of proved reserves in preference to the more liberal established reserves computational base.

On the futures side, board procedure is more debatable. In the past the method employed has been premised on the predictive value (assumed) of a ten-year moving average of discovery trends in conventional production. On the strength of this the board has contended that reasonably confident predictions might be made with respect to gas likely to be discovered in the future from these same conventional areas.

The weaknesses of this procedure are obvious. As applied, the board has paid no attention to the climbing incremental costs of discovery, development and production. Because of this the board has chosen to ignore the fact that generally trend gas is economically speaking of less value than the current inventories that are being released periodically for the export market. In addition, because the resource base being exploited is finite, as a practical matter the sheer geophysical attractiveness of the conventional zones has to decline. At some point this will reach the stage where little, if any, work will take place. While trend increments may have demonstrably conformed to some of the early board estimates, the sheer level of effort (and cost) has also risen quite substantially as an average, and inevitably both the amount of investment and the trend of discovery will fall off, if only by reason of the diminished physical (and commercial return) prospects of the conventional zones. Here, once more, the board procedures as applied have tended towards a highly simplified view of what is in fact a complicated problem.

However, while board procedures laboured under large weaknesses in the predictive realm, the actual role of the future reserves calculation has never been clear vis-à-vis export approval, and was, with recent revisions to procedures, more or less displaced by a complex future deliverability formula.

Export Determination
Early board procedures to safeguard domestic market requirements for natural gas were on a number of occasions both misapplied and ultimately unsuccessful. For example, in 1971 the NEB had to acknowledge the existence of a foreseeable deficit in Canada's supplies. The regulators had simply released too much gas for export, frequently under highly debatable price conditions, and for long periods of time into the future. The board had been too optimistic about the industry's finding rate, and repeatedly turned a blind eye to both relative cost factors and the deteriorating deliverability position that was later to seem so important. By 1975, Canada's potential supply crisis was beginning to assume frightening dimensions, and the board was obliged at least to examine how best to apportion the prospective shortages between export and domestic markets. The board also considered lengthy submissions concerning revised procedures that might better ensure adequate levels of protection in terms of both reserve deliverability and the quantities of gas held for future market

needs. As for exports, in 1975 there was no real urgency to arrive at a final resolution as to which set of procedures ought to be adopted. Future export applications remained at this point purely hypothetical in view of the decidedly unfavourable demand and supply balance that prevailed.

However, during the Northern Pipeline Hearings[31] it became clear that an upswing in conventional discovery trends had materially improved the reserve outlook. This, coupled with a moderated rate of demand growth (that necessarily accompanied the obstacles to expansion of the TransCanada Pipeline system), suggested increased scope for new exports. Indeed, the brightened outlook immeasurably weakened the case for a western Arctic natural gas pipeline. The board in 1978 felt that circumstances warranted propounding a new set of export procedures.

There were additional factors that had a bearing upon the export issue. The NEB's 1976 approval of the Foothills (Yukon) application for a pipeline[32] following the Alaska Highway had put to rest a decade's controversy about which project would receive a green light. But it also marked the beginning of a much more substantial controversy: namely, the terms under which the Canadian portion of the pipeline could be actually built. The application sanctioned by the board was largely hypothetical in form. Major elements, including financing, markets, environment, engineering and costs to completion, were left unresolved. At various points throughout the proceeding the project has been in doubt, as indeed it was in 1982. By late 1977 and early 1978, the board was mindful of the project's shaky status. There was a widespread belief within the ranks of government and industry that the export of more Canadian gas might provide needed support for the Alaska Highway project through a so-called "pre-build" of the southern portion of the line. The producers and Alberta also argued for an increase in allowable exports to maintain the brisk pace of industry exploratory activity.

Against this climate the board felt that it had to arrive at new export procedures. That the formula ultimately adopted would facilitate more exports in the future appeared to some to be a foregone conclusion. Indeed, the board ultimately adopted procedures that proved highly favourable to the producing industry's desire to export more Canadian gas.

The procedures adopted (and now in force) were reduced to three distinct phases.[33] The essential differences from the earlier methodology were that (a) deliverability was now a mandatory part of the export test, where before it was at best peripherally considered, and at worst ignored altogether; (b) the quantities of gas to be held in reserve for future Canadian needs were substantially less than that formerly stipulated; and (c) the discretionary power given the board to consider extraneous factors was enlarged. In short, the scope for export applications was increased both in a purely mathematical sense, and as regards the range of potential justifications that could be presented to the board. The details of the new procedures follow.

- Current Deliverability — As noted, the first phase of the board's examination of a proposed export involves an assessment of current deliverability. At issue here is a solitary question. Having in view the deliverability requirements of present Canadian and export customers over the next five years, is it possible to deliver to the proposed American buyers? Assuming sufficient field capability is demonstrated, then there is a "deemed surplus" in deliverability, all or some of which can be the subject of an export application.

- Current Requirements — The deliverability test does not involve a determination of the quantity of gas that might be allowed by the board. This issue is resolved through a calculation of current reserves according to a formula known as 25 A 1 (which involves multiplying the current year's domestic and export market needs by a factor of 25 to produce a total which is in turn subtracted from the most recent assessment of total established conventional reserves). As applied, the test must produce a positive number in order for the application to proceed further. But whether or not the entire difference between the current established reserves and the quantity indicated by the 25 A 1 requirements test is exportable depends not only upon the current deliverability test described above, but also upon a futures calculation.

- Future Deliverability — The future deliverability calculation is made highly problematic by reason of the substantial scope for regulatory discretion that it involves. Here the board attempts to assess deliverability over a decade from established reserves in both the conventional areas of production as well as the frontier. Such an assessment is complex and subject to extreme uncertainty.

First, a decade is a very long time in the context of accurately predicting deliverability. Ultimately a production history is the most useful source upon which projections can be developed. But, even in those areas where there is a relatively full history to draw upon, deliverability profiles nonetheless involve a great many subjective judgments. The recent revisions that have been necessary with respect to deliverability from Waterton and Kaybob South amply illustrate the dangers of relying too heavily upon such projections, notwithstanding an extensive production performance history.

Second, the inclusion of trend gas in the conventional zones plus frontier gas guarantees an even higher subjective quality. As a general rule of thumb, the degree of risk varies in inverse proportions with the quantity of actual production data on hand. Thus, the confidence limits in respect of undiscovered gas or unproduced discoveries in remote areas must by definition be extreme.

Third, there is the problem of crediting frontier reserves as if they were on a par in a value sense with conventional supplies. Clearly, southern-based sources of supply are more readily accessible to Canadian markets by virtue of being within easy reach of existing transmission facilities. To credit both southern and frontier reserves together involves a risk of the board once again following its past practice of inviting industry to build a case for a theoretical deliverability surplus which will only result in early export of conventional gas, which in turn condemns future Canadian consumers to relying upon the most distant, costly and uncertain sources earlier than would otherwise be necessary.

Conclusions and Recommendations

The National Energy Board technically has the statutory power to regulate Canadian energy resource development comprehensively throughout the country. But this is, on the basis of historical experience at least, clearly not a statement that has any basis in reality. The board has often remained passive with respect to its advisory functions in face of circumstances that demanded a comprehensive review of overall supply strategy in both the petroleum and gas sectors. In the areas of export and facilities approval, the board has consistently adhered to the position that its main duties lie in responding to applications that are first conceived of and advanced by the private sector. No apparent consideration appears ever to have been given to the formulation of a generalized development and export strategy, or to the relationships that may exist between oil, gas and hydroelectric power production. No effort was given to the deliberate promotion of east-west transmission facilities, the deliberate promotion of domestic market growth in any area other than natural gas, or the implementation of regulatory policies that would aid in maintaining long-term stable energy costs.

The NEB was condemned to the discharge of an impossibly broad and imprecise mandate. Its response was to narrow its focus to a degree that history appears to have demonstrated to have been inappropriate.

Since 1973 the board has had to face a rapidly changing climate within both government and industry. Under the circumstances, its performance has in some respects proven quite remarkable. Its workload has expanded immeasurably. It had four chairmen in the period 1973 to 1980. It has conducted a series of important hearings, including the longest and most complicated in Canada's history (the Northern Pipeline Hearings). The board has been assaulted publicly, studied and extensively criticized by both government and academics, and forced to cope with an aggressive and oftentimes difficult series of "public interest" interventions, as well as being liable to a series of court challenges. Throughout, its demeanour has remained consistently courteous, and its efforts unquestionably sincere. But the quality of its substantive performance has been less impressive, particularly in the realm of export control.

It is useful to examine some factors that might explain the difficulty that the board had in developing and maintaining a workable set of general export criteria to protect future Canadian energy needs. First, the history leading to the board's creation indicates that petroleum, gas and electrical exports involved a delicate and highly complicated balance between an array of conflicting national policy objectives that included (from time to time) defence, security for domestic markets, western economic expansion, secondary development in the petrochemical field, development of Canadian hydrocarbon potential, and so on. The historical record is clearly revealing about the inability of the line agencies of government to cope effectively with the sophistications of the issues involved. Thus the board was styled as a specialized, largely independent tribunal charged with the duty of making a first foray into a basically uncharted sphere for government regulation. Because of the intricacies involved, the activities of the board were bound to assume a somewhat mysterious air for both the public and the government that was responsible for its creation. Thus the board's analyses and recommendations were often taken on faith until circumstances implied a need to do otherwise.

If a single factor has to be chosen by way of explanation for the limited success of the board in discharging its broad mandate, the best item would appear to be the fact that the private sector held a virtual monopoly over much of the data and expertise basic to the board's work. Few outside of the immediate ranks of industry were in a position to question such basic assumptions as the theoretical correctness of the volumetric method of reserve assessment, or the proposition that one Mcf (million cubic feet) of gas was worth an amount exactly equal to another Mcf regardless of the time or location of discovery. The fact that the board had to rely upon industry-developed data almost exclusively, and had to draw much of its personnel from the private sector, guaranteed a high degree of sympathy between regulators and regulated. At times this sympathy may have prevented the searching examination of fundamentals that the public interest required.

As the board alone acts under a statutory obligation to control the problem, it must now accept at least part of the responsibility for the development of the present situation. But it must also be said that many of the interests with the largest stakes in board export decisions also failed utterly either to perceive and/or articulate positions and thus did little to help the NEB. The provincial power utilities, including Ontario Hydro and the British Columbia Hydro Power Authority, failed to make use of the NEB hearings as a means of maintaining adequate access to natural gas supplies. The same might be said of the major distribution companies and major pipeline companies serving Canadian markets. The domination that the producing and exporting industry appears to have enjoyed over the regulators was maintained in part through the default of other potentially countervailing interests.

The NEB's historical record may seem a weak foundation for the expanded role that this study suggests is necessary for a proper discharge of its statutory mandate. As suggested above, to some degree the board's views of its own powers were conditioned by the highly specialized nature of its work, its historical independence from government, and the fact that the producing industry alone appeared interested and communicated regularly with it. Neither government nor the public were major participants until the events of 1973 when the political relevance of energy was perhaps forever established.

Even today NEB decision-making is achieved through hearings which are universally dominated by the industry being regulated. It is the industry, most usually applicants, that largely influence the pace and direction of a proceeding. Their briefs are prepared, presented and defended by an array of experts backed by legal counsel. Where necessary, the same resources are available for the preparation of cross-examination of opposing evidence. By way of distinct contrast, conservation and other public interest groups are incapable of matching the resources that are available to industry and as a result fall rapidly behind. The board's attitude towards the non-industry briefs has from time to time ranged from tolerant bemusement to occasional impatience. Indeed, the board's attitudes are not unreasonable within the often compelling sociology of an individual proceeding. But, on a larger scale, the issues that have been advanced by various public interest groups have often proved to be the most substantially significant of any put forward. The board has often appeared blind to the distinction that exists between a relevant argument couched in amateurish terms and advanced by unpaid, non-legal volunteers as opposed to a poor rationale, polished in form and presented by highly competent professionals. The result over time has been less and less public interest participation in board proceedings and a growing cynicism about the board's sense of procedural fairness.

From the board's standpoint other factors have militated against encouraging more public interest group participation, the main element being the enormously increased workload. A growing sense of urgency has compelled a degree of procedural rigour in board proceedings that has in turn produced so heavy a daily workload for serious participants that effective non-industry briefs are almost out of the question.

In short, the public interest groups were in many cases ill-equipped to advance effectively the important issues they put before the NEB. Because their motivations were public spirited as opposed to pecuniary, the public interest spokesmen were viewed with distrust and frequently accused of being both presumptuous and overly pious. This, coupled with amateurish presentations, encouraged short shrift being given to their arguments in many instances.

The National Energy Board Act stipulates in favour of public hearings with the precise ambition of facilitating a broad examination of the issues inherent to a given application. Complete industry domination of these proceedings unnecessarily impairs the NEB's obligation to apprise itself fully of the public interest issues involved in a given decision. Generally, the broader the base of evidence before the board, the more probable it is that the decision reached will reflect an overall assessment of the inherent public interest issues. The board should not, where possible, be left in the position of having to second-guess the conflicts and dilemmas that are basic to its jurisdiction simply because its own procedures have had the effect of excluding relevant material. It is therefore recommended that a series of measures be adopted to ensure that the board has broader access to a range of well-polished and thoroughly considered "untraditional" perspectives in its public hearings.

Recommendation 9. Public Funding Should be Made Available to Public Interest Groups

The question of government subsidization of public interest groups has been the subject of some debate in the past. Mr. Justice Berger's inquiry concerning the Mackenzie Valley Corridor benefited substantially from the briefs and arguments of well-funded public interest representation. The NEB in its Northern Pipeline Hearings did not follow a similar path, and indeed was prepared to do no more than provide three copies of the transcript of proceedings on a daily loan basis to be shared by more than twice the number of public interest intervenors.

In discussions between various senior civil servants and ministers and public interest groups it became apparent that a funding policy was hamstrung on a number of major points of concern. First, there was the "floodgates" argument. According to this theory, public funding would generate wide interest in participation at public hearings and would mire them in endless controversy. However, on the basis of historical experience it would seem an extremely remote possibility that this would ever be the result of public funding. There is simply no evidence whatever that supports the notion of a latent backlog of public interest representatives that are held back by want of funds alone. As the Berger inquiry revealed, serious participation is an exceptionally wearing experience, and not usually highly remunerative for the participants.

A second concern of government has been the fear that more public interest group involvement before the NEB would unnecessarily add to its workload and delay its decision-making processes. On this point there is little doubt that issues of substance would be tested more fully, but this is not the same thing as delay for delay's sake. On the contrary, once again on the strength of past experience, a number of very real weaknesses in applications that deserved careful consideration from the board were exposed by the so-called "public interest sector." Adequate funding in this sense would make the various groups far more efficient in productively testing material put before the tribunal. If there have been difficulties in the past, they have primarily arisen from inadequate opportunity to prepare, which in some cases drove the various groups to attempt to delay in order to buy more time.

A third area of concern is the complex argument that the public interest function properly belongs to government generally and the board in particular, and therefore to support the so-called "public interest groups" would be tantamount to an acknowledgement of failure on the part of the regulators. In this connection, the very term "public interest group" is somewhat unfortunate. Many of the interests lumped into this category do not presume to speak to what is in fact the ultimate public interest in a given application, any more than does an application or industry intervenor. Instead they reflect secular concerns such as wildlife habitat preservation, the native people, the cause of economic nationalism, various church groups, and so on. All that any party can offer is a particular set of biases developed from a specialized vantage point. The final and broad judgment as to what is and is not in the public's best interest still very much lies in the hands of the tribunal, and for this reason there is no basis in logic for denying funding simply because a group has been labelled by media, and perhaps by the board, as being part of the public interest sector. In common usage, all this label amounts to is that the spokesmen are not employed by either the oil and gas industry or the government.

For these reasons it is recommended that the federal government establish a funding program to enable more effective public interest representation before the NEB. The government should insist upon the designation of umbrella groups with responsibility for coordination between the various non-industry interests in particular hearings, and where necessary should refuse funding to prevent needless redundancy of effort.

Recommendation 10. The Hearing Process Should be Restructured

The capacity of the regulators to evaluate the public interest is sometimes limited by a large lack of argument and data relevant to the making of a particular decision. Time and again the history of various regulatory tribunals has reflected a propensity towards ultimate industry captivation. The causes of this phenomenon are not particularly mysterious, nor is the process in any way an unnatural one. Regulatory bodies are created to contend with specific social and economic complexities in a particular activity. The ordinary branches of government, being preoccupied with the day-to-day affairs of the country, are unable to pay close enough heed to these issues. Furthermore, these very same complexities oblige the regulators to amass expertise and evolve effective standards of control where the sole source of knowledge lies within the very people being regulated.

The dialogue that evolves is often unique in terms of language, and the issues discussed are of immediate interest to a small community. Often, a sense of mutual interest rapidly develops between regulated and regulator.

The regulation of Canadian energy resource development has at times seemed as much impaired by this process of industry cooperation as has been true of the more notorious U.S. examples frequently cited in the contemporary literature. The National Energy Board was created with broad powers and responsibility, but with little meaningful direction from government. In 1959 there was not a great deal of public attention paid to the broad energy issue, and board proceedings were rapidly, if not immediately, dominated by the producing sector of the oil and gas industry.

Public interest representation was not a significant factor until 1974 when the first major natural gas re-evaluation was commissioned. Prior to this, such representations as had been heard by the board were sporadic, involving either individuals acting alone, or single conservation or consuming groups. By 1974 there were indications that as many as a dozen public interest organizations might be prepared to seek intervenor status before the Mackenzie Valley pipeline hearing. But even at their zenith, the public interest groups were seen by both industry and the board as being enigmatic. At no point were they able to come to the process on an equal footing with the industry. While, as suggested in recommendation 9 above, public interest funding will undoubtedly help improve the quality and, with time, the acceptance of public interest briefs, it would be too much to assume that this sector alone can cause a major change in regulatory perception of the public interest.

A durable improvement will arguably necessitate a restructuring of board proceedings to ensure the regulators are exposed to as full a spectrum of the conflicts as the circumstances will allow. To take one illustration, as noted, the oil and gas producing industry was able to achieve a dominant position in respect of the NEB's early decision-making that arguably has proved to be at the ultimate expense of many large consuming interests. The consuming sectors were not well organized, nor well represented at board hearings for the most part. Thus little attention was given to the impact of increasing the price of either oil or gas, and the evidence brought forth by the producers of the implications of higher prices remained relatively unchallenged by the very people most apt to be affected.

In short, like other regulatory tribunals, the National Energy Board has been essentially a victim of circumstance. The oil and gas industry was the best technically equipped, most thoroughly prepared, and most consistently interested voice that was heard by the tribunal. Consumer groups, industry associations and public bodies, including the provinces and provincial utilities, were less familiar with the issues and less inclined to make use of the forum offered by the board. By virtual default, many early decisions were heavily influenced by the industry being regulated, and the particular contention that the public interest paramountly lay with expansion and growth in the oil and gas producing sector assumed the status of "conventional wisdom." Even today the board continues to be acutely aware of producer-related problems, more so than is evident with respect to the long-term effects of its decisions upon consuming interests. Almost no serious published analysis has ever been received by the board concerning the industrial, employment and consumption effects of higher prices. As noted, the board has gone as far as to revise protection criteria in order to release more gas for export as a means of boosting short-term producer cash flow.

Without an effort to redress the present imbalance in the hearing process, board decision-making will remain somewhat one-dimensional for the reasons discussed. A restructuring of the hearing process through the inclusion of a broader range of intervenors would help to expand the evidence (and conflicts) before the tribunal, and ensure a more rigorous testing of the issues basic to the public interest determinations of the board. In this regard, it is recommended that measures be adopted to ensure that the following parties assume an active role in all major board proceedings.

- Through the participation of the National Energy Marketing Commission,* the board will be obliged to evaluate hard evidence with respect to market effects, transmission factors and overall domestic requirements at a level of detail that has not been a characteristic of past proceedings. Moreover, the National Energy Marketing Commission, as a public tribunal with its own statutory mandate, will be able to speak with a broader perspective and go beyond what is the most commercially convenient decision having regard to the commercial interests of private companies. As a result, the NEB will be able to address the broad impact of a given decision against the background of a more fully articulated

---

*This body is discussed in detail in the following chapter, as is the relationship proposed between it and the NEB.

domestic interest. In the particular fields of export licensing and advisory proceedings this should be of substantial benefit to the board, most particularly at a time when the growing vertical integration between the producing and transmission sectors threatens to jeopardize an already deficient hearing process still further.

- Petro-Canada, the Canada Development Corporation, Canertech, etc. should intervene before the National Energy Board wherever there are issues to be discussed which touch upon their respective spheres of operation. Sporadic interventions, motivated strictly on the basis of immediate commercial interest, may only undermine the real advantages that can result if the board is able to consider the longer-term interests of those Crown corporations active in the field. Because the public-sector companies operate through statutory mandates, their view of the oil and gas sector is often based on a longer perspective compared to the shorter-term views of the larger private and often foreign-dominated companies.

  But while these firms are statutorily mandated, they should not be obliged to coordinate strategy with the proposed National Energy Marketing Corporation or with the National Energy Board. Quite to the contrary, conflict should usually define their respective appearances in view of the differences in their respective statutory circumstances.

- The Petroleum Import Compensation Board, the Petroleum Incentive Board, etc. should all be entitled, if not actively encouraged, to present evidence and argument formally before the board in their own right. The board from time to time must consider the import picture as well as price incentive factors. Because there are, or may be, active public agencies in these areas, the board should take their views into account. In fairness to all parties, informal communications should be discouraged and views should be expressed in the context of formal presentations at board hearings. Certainly this manner of proceeding would be more informative for all concerned.

Recommendation 11.   The Board Should Overhaul the Presently Applied Export Criteria

The procedures now applied to determine export applications have been described. Despite their recent revision, board procedures continue to labour under substantial uncertainties. To some extent analytical doubt is inevitable, given that future requirements and future discovery trends must by definition continue to remain unknowns. But, in other instances, the board has opted for procedures that amplify rather than mitigate the level of uncertainty. The following discussion suggests how existing board procedures might be amended and, in the writer's view, materially improved.

Elimination of "Surplus" Terminology
NEB export approvals are presently conditional upon the finding of a so-called "exportable surplus." This terminology is highly misleading and has the effect of obscuring the true issues in a given export decision. Notionally speaking, the likelihood of a surplus existing at any point in time is remote. First, the resource being exported is finite in an absolute sense. Second, when one adds commercial factors into the calculation, the exploitable base of supply is even more limited. Indeed, the inexpensive and highly accessible gas that was committed to export customers in the past has clearly proved not to have been surplus at all by any common-sense definition of that term. Domestic market requirements have developed to a point where all of the conventional gas that has been discovered can be absorbed, particularly if the fuel conversion objectives of the NEP are pursued in future. The fact that exports were approved in the past has only resulted in the importation of cost escalations and potential deliverability worries, if not outright shortfalls, at an earlier point than would have been true otherwise. These factors can hardly be described as symptoms of a past glut or gas "surplus." Stripped to essentials, the board in deeming gas to be "surplus" is doing no more than deciding that its view of the circumstances warrants the commitment of gas to present-day American buyers in preference to future Canadian customers. The issue of obvious significance is the articulation by the board of the circumstances that it found persuasive and not the artificial conclusion that gas is not required by the domestic market.

With this discussion in mind, it is recommended that the board establish an export test that revolves around the determination of an "exportable supply component" rather than an "exportable surplus." This apparently minor alteration in the language employed provides a single, and quite major, advantage to the extent that it will both eliminate public confusion and call into question the true reasons of substance in support of a given export approval or rejection, rather than simply highlight a misleading and entirely arbitrary mathematical judgment.

Revision of Domestic Market Protection Factor
In its 1978 procedure review, the board settled upon a 25 A 1 domestic market protection formula. This revision, as applied, reserves less gas for future Canadian use than did the former 25 A 4 (or twenty-five times domestic requirements four years hence) formula. The amendment appears to have been directed simply at increasing the so-called "exportable surplus" and allowing a greater quantity of gas to flow across the border. The brief in favour of this step was no more complicated than the desire to alleviate the alleged cash flow problems of Alberta producers, encourage the completion of the Alaska gas transmission system, and create a healthier climate for more industry investment. In the meantime, the National Energy Program has laid great emphasis upon more intense use of natural gas in lieu of oil, both in traditional areas of gas service and in new market regions, including Atlantic Canada. As a result, the application of a 25 A 1 formula will misstate what, on the strength of formal government policy, is going to be a much expanded market. Indeed, even the 25 A 4 test would be unsatisfactory to the extent that more expansion can be expected in the domestic market after 1985.

It is recommended that the board conform to the direction of government policy and assess (and protect) Canadian requirements on the basis of market growth over a fifteen-year period (at a minimum). It follows that any arbitrary "flat curve" that is the result of an application of an equally arbitrary formulation of demand should be rejected forthwith.

Examination of an Export Credit System
Much of the impetus for gas export has recently come from producers who made commercial judgments concerning domestic market growth and the trend of gas discovery in the conventional play, both of which proved inaccurate. The slow rate of growth and the unexpectedly favourable discovery trend created a so-called "supply bubble" and, with it, genuinely difficult conditions for producers who had relied upon a ready market outlet. Their claims for relief were in part addressed by the NEP's proposed Natural Gas Bank which was critically considered in chapter 2.

The cash flow problems of the conventional producers imply a national misallocation of capital resources. Rather than "too much gas" in any absolute sense, Canada must instead contend with the short-term results of an early over-commitment of exploratory capital in the conventional reserve areas. There is, in short, a timing problem, with too much current deliverability for a limited domestic and export market. With this in mind, the drive to increase allowable exports, coupled with the higher producer returns from export sales, plus the movement of rigs and survey equipment out of the conventional plays, is a completely natural consequence.

Much public attention has focused upon the southward flight of rigs and crews. While maintaining a high level of domestic exploration capability may be desirable, as an objective in itself it is subordinate to the maintenance of adequate conventional gas stocks. Premature alienation of gas into export markets as a means of "subsidizing" the retention of drilling capacity would in effect involve making the rigs more important than the gas that they discover. It would also as a policy very quickly lead Canada into a situation much like that affecting Canadian bank interest rates. Domestic policies would have to be tailored to ensure a financial advantage in order to compete successfully with the U.S. for rigs and drilling crews. And all of this would occur in face of the reality that premature rig activity involves a draw upon capital resources that could be better applied in other investment spheres.

Nonetheless, it may be in Canada's best interests in specific circumstances to attempt to take some advantage of the premium incentive that gas export markets offer domestic producers. Under conditions where it is in the country's best interests to encourage more conventional exploration (such as might be true if a major frontier project were delayed, or if for some other reason conventional supplies were needed over a longer period), a firm export component representing a percentage of discoveries might be offered over a specific (and always prospective) period of time. For example, conventional producers might be told that one-third of any discoveries of "new gas" found between March 31, 1982 and January 1, 1983 could be exported as of right, assuming concurrence from the relevant provincial conservation authorities.

Such a system offers advantages. It is result-oriented, depending entirely upon what a producer/explorer actually finds, as opposed to the more usual acceptance of what might later be found if exports were opened up today. It is simple and short-circuits the necessity of elaborate and complex export hearings after the gas has been discovered (whether or not prior hearings should be held around the particular "export percentage of discoveries" standard offered is, however, an open issue that may merit board consideration). And finally, such a system forces an early concrete relationship to be drawn

94

by the board between the decision to allow exports and the particular national gains to be served.

The system is, however, useful only to the extent that it is wisely applied. The duration of the "export allowables" should be in every case held to the minimum commercial period feasible under the circumstances. Moreover, policing will have to be strict in view of the production uncertainties associated with new discoveries, and to prevent initial reserves in place being exaggerated in order to boost export allowables artificially. Provincial cooperation will likely prove critical here. Finally, the board should initiate such a system experimentally, perhaps on a limited area basis, with an eye towards evaluating the risks involved before a broad application takes place.

The All-Energy Approach

In the past the NEB has compartmentalized Canadian energy problems in a manner that has proven unrealistic. Its early work centred on natural gas, and detailed effort was devoted towards the evolution of a complex (albeit imperfect) system of export controls. During this period, oil was not looked at in any detail, nor were oil exports controlled. It was only in 1972 that the board developed an unease about Canada's producing status, and it was not until 1974 that the board finally imposed rudimentary export controls. More recently the board has considered, but again not regulated, coal exports. Once more, coal requirements in the future are a source of uncertainty in view of the NEP's off-oil targets and the risk of an oil import supply disruption in the interim.

The board has recently made some effort to update its overall assessment of total Canadian energy needs, and has called for submissions from industry and elsewhere in aid of its analysis. But it is a long way from successfully incorporating an optimum mix of energy targets in its current procedures. As noted above, even in the natural gas export sphere, board procedures with respect to domestic market protection appear at odds with the long-term objectives of established government policy.

If the board is to take account of the comprehensive approach of the NEP in respect of inter-modal energy targets, it is clear the tribunal will have to develop an implementation strategy. For this to be accomplished successfully, it will be necessary for the regulators to screen applications forcefully and check their decisions for compatibility with the broader all-energy goals. In this context, the proceedings discussed with reference to energy investment screening would prove a useful addition to the board's overall responsibility (see discussion under recommendation 5 in chapter 2).

The NEB should also periodically review the feasibility of the general energy targets, and where necessary make recommendations with respect to revisions to existing programs that may be advisable, and suggest other measures that might help sustain the effort towards achieving an optimal energy mix. Investment in improved interprovincial power transmission facilities might be an example of the latter type of recommendation. In this fashion the board might be more systematic in its approach towards its broad mandate over Canadian energy resource development.

Recommendation 12.   Board Certification Should be Required for All Future Nuclear Power Plant Projects
This chapter has argued for a far broader role for the National Energy Board. Ultimately, the tribunal's usefulness will lie in its capacity to assist with policy development and implementation at a broad was well as a particular level. Where before now it has given short shrift to comparative energy analysis, in the future it ought to address the full panorama of energy alternatives and evaluate workable priorities for their exploitation.

Nuclear power is frequently touted as a major Canadian energy alternative. The nuclear power issue raises difficult controversies, including both cost and safety, that are not addressed here. But the overall issue of the comparative value of the nuclear option must be subjected to careful and regular appraisal from time to time. With this objective in mind, it is recommended that board certification should be a precondition for the addition of any future operational nuclear facilities.

However, the jurisdiction given the board in this regard should be limited. The NEB should not be required to address siting and safety questions which are already liable to regulatory supervision at both the federal and provincial levels of government. The NEB's approval should be confined to issues that relate directly to the cost of facilities, and the impact of certification in terms of the scheduling of other energy priorities. Any prospective export components that may be built into a new plant should also be reviewed at this juncture, again in an attempt to ensure that each new energy undertaking represents the most productive allocation of capital resources possible in the circumstances.

A National Energy Marketing Commission?

4

A series of recommendations have been made that involve adding to the present structure of regulatory controls over energy. These recommendations have included creating a new Petroleum Import Control Board for the overall management of imports of petroleum (which would include detailed state supervision over the purchasing, storage, allocation and pricing of future petroleum imports), the implementation of an energy investment screening process, and wholesale reform of the National Energy Board. But such changes, while substantial in their own right, still go only part of the way towards establishing an array of controls sufficient to cope with the difficult transition to higher costs and periods of regional energy shortages that may lie ahead.

Canada has diverse energy sources available to different markets under an equally diverse set of regulatory and commercial conditions. For example, petroleum and natural gas prices have in the past been regulated by the federal government through the medium of federal-provincial agreement. Electricity rates within the provinces are, by contrast, liable only to provincial control. Coal prices in intra- or interprovincial markets are not regulated.

The transmission systems in use are equally subject to differing treatment, depending upon both the type of system involved (e.g., pipelines, rail transport or highway transport) and whether it is intra- or interprovincial and/or international. Intraprovincial oil and gas lines remain under provincial jurisdiction, falling (theoretically) only under federal control when they connect to systems that serve other Canadian or foreign markets. Power transmission lines are also under provincial jurisdiction, although once again NEB approval is necessary whenever they extend beyond provincial boundaries. Neither the interprovincial movement of coal nor the movement of hydrocarbons through rail or highway networks are subject to central regulation. In brief, the current federal regulatory controls over energy and energy transportation are somewhat spotty.

Moreover, the degree of federal control is also uneven in terms of the nature of the jurisdiction that is exercised in those instances where there is no doubt as to the federal government's constitutional power to regulate. For example, in the sphere of pipeline and transmission line certification, the applications themselves are brought forward on behalf of the commercial operators and/or provincial utilities concerned. As discussed in chapter 3, the NEB in such cases is able to do little more than recommend marginal changes, with the main outlines of a given proposal, as well as its timing, firmly under the control of its advocate. What this in turn means is that such important questions as the overall balance of consumption between different energy forms and the total mix of transmission capacity into the various Canadian energy markets are both determined by independent application sponsors, without any consideration necessarily being given to what in the long run may be ideal.

In the National Energy Program the federal government expressed clear targets for different types of energy resources consumption. It is contended here that, to accomplish these targets, the federal government must exercise more affirmative power over the development and advancement of major new systems, as well as imposing more intimate control over the management of those systems already in place.

The NEP also set forth clear policy objectives with respect to energy pricing over the next decade and beyond. Once again, comprehensive regulation of energy development, transmission and pricing will be in order if these objectives are to be ultimately accomplished.

This chapter examines the usefulness of establishing a federal energy marketing commission as a means of acquiring the needed degree of ongoing central control that is necessary to realize the energy objectives described in both the NEP and, indeed, this study. Canada has had a lengthy history with national marketing boards as vehicles aimed at bringing difficult economic-regulatory problems to heel. The establishment of a wheat board is often cited as one of the more successful ventures in this regard. But, however logical the case in favour of comprehensive regulatory control over wheat markets might at one time have been, it pales in comparison with the potential controversies attached to Canada's current energy marketing problems. As was true of the earlier example, Canada may once again be forced to appeal to central jurisdictional powers in order to acquire control through regulation along the lines discussed in this chapter.

98

The Constitutional Basis

The importance of oil and gas to the nation's economy and the welfare of the population as a whole is beyond issue. Possibly of even greater significance are the terms under which both commodities are made available to the country. Without free access to indigenous oil and gas supplies, Canada could hardly claim to possess the economic integration that the Economic Council of Canada recently termed the "*sine qua non* of Canadian federalism."

> Without a commitment to an integrated or common market, i.e., "a single market within which goods, services, labour, and capital may move freely without impediments created by public authorities" (A.E. Safarian, *Canadian Federalism and Economic Integration* [Ottawa: Information Canada, 1974], p. 2) there can be no meaningful commitment to a unified country. Furthermore there are, in Canada's case, very practical reasons that should reinforce that commitment. As Safarian has argued, "the large size of countries with whom we must compete and the formation of very large customs unions and free trade areas elsewhere in the world make it essential for Canada to derive maximum advantage from its own relatively small internal market."[1]

As a result of the dispute between Ottawa and Alberta concerning oil pricing, Canadian oil production was arbitrarily restrained for an extended period. In response, there was a costly increase in Canadian petroleum import volumes at a time when the Canadian balance of payments was a particularly pressing concern.

At the core of the disagreement between Ottawa and Alberta was a fundamental challenge to the very notion of unrestricted internal free trade within the present constitutional framework. Having appropriate regard to the magnitude of both the fiscal and political stakes involved, the importance of quickly implementing a more orderly central regulatory scheme should by now be clear.

The constitutional support for a larger federal role in the particular context of marketing boards and market regulation has generally expanded over the last two decades. But while it is now more or less beyond doubt that the federal government technically has wide powers in the marketing field, Ottawa has been to some extent politically conditioned by the long history of judicial rebukes during the first five decades of this century, and has accordingly exercised its powers sparingly. More importantly perhaps, the provinces have been encouraged as a result of this reticence to expect a minimum of interference. Today, to take full advantage of the technically wide scope of jurisdiction under the heads of constitutional power discussed below, the federal government will have to overcome the well-established custom that special or unusual circumstances will alone politically justify an increased federal presence in areas that traditionally have been within provincial jurisdiction.

It should be noted in passing that Canada's position is somewhat unusual compared with other federal states. In the United States, the selection of the appropriate level for regulatory intervention has often appeared to turn upon practical considerations more than trite formalities or traditions.

Interestingly, U.S. central powers were constrained as were Canada's by a half-century of adverse Supreme Court decisions. Roosevelt's selective appointments to the U.S. Supreme Court increased the level of sympathy for federal initiatives and may ultimately have helped gradually to reverse this trend. But the judicial reversal in attitude could be as much credited to a growing awareness that federal control often improved the economic environment within which many of the regulated enterprises had to operate. Thus today most national markets are well within the constitutional reach of the U.S. federal government, at least in theory if not in practice. As one author observed, while this regulation may not always be economically coherent in origin or scope:

> . . .there is a political coherence in it all; namely, those who have sufficient political influence to bring about a market modification in their favour have done so — and they usually have done so through the medium of the central government with its present-day control of national markets.
>
> This is not to say significant markets are not still controlled by the states. Indeed they are. . .
>
> On the whole, markets are national nowadays and hence economic regulation or the modification of market outcomes is national.

In Canada there is no real doubt that energy is marketed on a national scale. The entire transportation infrastructure is geared towards bridging what are usually long distances between production sites and markets. Only in Ontario and Quebec does one find large-scale production and consumption of indigenous supplies that do not entail interprovincial or international transmission. But even here, Ontario and Quebec are both critically dependent upon oil and gas supplies imported through the two major national pipeline systems of Interprovincial and TransCanada. The inherent nature of Canada's energy market and the dispute between Alberta and Ottawa are both compelling reasons for centralized management. The production restraints imposed by the province of Alberta have offered an effective historical illustration of the potential chaos that unrestrained provincial control would appear to promise in future.

Three principal sources of jurisdiction will be examined as possible avenues under which a national marketing plan might be justified, given Canada's present constitution. To some extent all three are interrelated, but, in the interest of clearer analysis, they have been treated as nominally independent. They are: the federal authority under the ''regulation of trade and commerce power'';[2] the general power ''to make laws for the Peace, Order and Good Government of Canada'';[3] and the declaratory power under section 92(10) (c) of the British North America Act.

The Regulation of Trade and Commerce

The trade and commerce power has been the source of much confusion in the past. The most immediate difficulty lay in the reconciling of whatever interpretation might be given to the operative words ''trade'' and ''commerce'' with the balance of power set forth under sections 91 and 92 of the British North America Act. In particular, the reason the trade and commerce power could not be given an unrestricted meaning could be found in the inescapable overlap with the provincial power over property and civil rights. The problem was a definitional one. ''Trade'' or ''commerce'' resulted from privately-made contracts that defined ''civil'' or private ''rights'' over ''property.'' This functional interdependence between trade and commerce on the one hand, and property and civil rights on the other, was the touchstone for never-ending constitutional confusion and doubt. Because common sense offered only dilemmas, the courts were driven to specialized definitions and principles in an effort to establish a workable line between the federal and provincial jurisdictions.

Through the application of the principle of ''mutual modification,'' the trade and commerce power was at first restricted in favour of a liberal interpretation of the provincial powers under property and civil rights. Indeed, the latter at one time assumed the status of a near ''residuary jurisdiction'' into which all those cases not specifically assigned to the federal government were in danger of being lumped. In one early case it was held that trade and commerce could be taken to include no more than:

> . . .political arrangements in regard to trade requiring the sanction of Parliament, regulation of trade in matters of inter-provincial concern, and it may be that they would include general regulation of trade affecting the whole dominion.[4]

For a period this decision was widely held to mean that the trade and commerce power would always yield in favour of provincial jurisdiction except where clear interprovincial, international or general trade and commerce questions were involved.

As a national "bright line" between property and civil rights on the one hand, and trade and commerce on the other, this definition left much to be desired. For example, the insurance industry (which had been the subject of the original controversy that led to the early case law supporting the provinces) involved usually more than one province, and was an industry whose health was of national concern given the importance of stable financial institutions that could support Canada's early growth and development. In this regard, the advantages of central regulatory control were obvious, but were considered unpersuasive by the Privy Council on at least two separate occasions.[5]

These cases represented the opening of an era which saw a humiliating reduction of the central government's jurisdiction under the trade and commerce power that at times seemed to reach absurd proportions. The low water mark of this trend could be found in the contention that trade and commerce lacked any independent content as a head of jurisdiction.[6] According to this view, trade and commerce could do no more than support other clearer heads of federal power. Thus, to take one example, trade and commerce might lie as an additional support for federal legislation passed to regulate interprovincial trade or to control the operation of an interprovincial work. But, according to this interpretation, trade and commerce would not provide any independent justification for federal legislation aimed at the control of general commercial ills (e.g., the control of monopolies and price regulation) because this would successfully touch the affairs of many industries which operated solely within individual provinces.

Early federal efforts to engage in market regulation involved the traversing of an obstacle-strewn path to say the very least. The most formidable early attempt to put in place market controls involved grain sales. Here, to finally overcome the constitutional niceties of the problem, the federal government was forced to resort to its declaratory power under section 92(10)(c) of the BNA Act which brought all of the intraprovincial grain elevators under the jurisdiction of Parliament "for the General Advantage of Canada." Otherwise, the fact of the elevators being within the individual provinces was sufficient to fatally flaw the regulatory scheme in its entirety.

There were subsequent agricultural product marketing causes during the period from 1937 to the 1950s[7] that confirmed the view that any inclusion of transactions that were capable of being completed entirely within an individual province (and therefore nominally under provincial regulatory jurisdiction) would represent a clear excess of jurisdiction on the part of the central government, and the entire scheme would collapse as a result. But in 1957[8] a break in the chain appeared when the Supreme Court suggested that transactions that involved both intra- and extraprovincial sales could not be so easily divided along purely jurisdictional lines, and that practical considerations instead might necessitate a single authority over both categories of transactions.

A year later the Supreme Court upheld a provision of the Canada Wheat Board Act which stipulated that all grain sales destined for markets outside of the province of production fell under the jurisdiction of the Canada Wheat Board.[9] More particularly, the Wheat Board was given the broad power to determine marketing terms and to distribute the proceeds received to the provincial producers.

An even more telling breakthrough occurred in 1959 when the Manitoba Court of Appeal held that the reach of the federal scheme included entirely local transactions involving the direct sale of provincially produced grains to local farmers.[10] On its face, the Canada Wheat Board Act applied. The logic here in favour of the Wheat Board was the organization and maintenance of a market quota system under which an attempt was made to provide equal access to all of Canada's producers. In other words, the regulatory scheme aimed at protecting individual producers through market controls. If a single producer could exceed a quota by increasing his intraprovincial sales, the entire fabric of the scheme was in danger of being undermined. For this reason, the Manitoba Court upheld the power of the board to regulate what otherwise might have been termed a purely local transaction. In response, the then Professor Bora Laskin wrote:

> The dominating consideration must have been that the sweep of the Act was supported by the economic facts — trade in wheat was, for Canada, essentially a matter of export and interprovincial movement. Realistically, then, any movement of wheat into marketing channels, be they intra-provincial or not, was a movement which could reasonably be subjected to a federal control scheme for the marketing of wheat.[11]

In short, the *Klassen* case represented a major turning away from the old line of Privy Council decisions which had seen the reduction of the trade and commerce power to what one academic had termed the "old forlorn hope."[12] As Laskin contended, a more functional approach had begun to supplant the earlier mechanical interpretive processes of the Privy Council. As a result, the utility of the trade and commerce power was considerably widened in the context of federal marketing regulatory schemes.

Klassen was in part confirmed in the *Caloil* v. *A.G. Canada* decision.[13] Here the issue was the power of the federal government (through the National Energy Board) to prohibit the transportation and sale of imported oil west of the Ottawa Valley. The federal government had in effect constructed an enormous oil marketing plan under which western producers were assured of a complete monopoly over all Canadian markets west of the Ottawa region. As Pigeon noted:

> . . .the policy intended to be implemented by the impugned enactment *is a control of the imports of a given commodity to foster the development and utilization of Canadian oil resources.* The restriction on the distribution of the imported product to a defined area is intended to reserve the market in other areas for the benefit of products from other parts of Canada. Therefore, the true character of the enactment appears to be an incident in the administration of an extraprovincial marketing scheme as in *Murphy* v. *C.P.R.* . . . Under the circumstances, *the interference with local trade, restricted as it is to an imported commodity is an integral part of the control of imports in the furtherance of an extraprovincial trade policy and cannot be termed "an unwarranted invasion of provincial jurisdiction."* (Emphasis added.)[14]

Thus, where before the incidental interference with a local transaction would be a flaw sufficient to destroy an entire federal regulatory scheme, the Supreme Court of Canada now reached what appeared to be the opposite view. Local transactions that were caught as a mere incident of an interprovincial or international marketing regulation scheme could now validly fall within federal control, should this be necessary to ensure the integrity of the federal plan. But in the *Caloil* case, as was true of previous decisions, the existence of interprovincial trade flows was the critical variable enabling the courts to support the overall structure. Indeed, in the particular context of energy marketing it is clear that there continues to be a very large interprovincial and international component, and for this reason federal regulatory jurisdiction would appear to be on safe ground so far as the present transmission infrastructure is concerned.

But the theory of trade and commerce set forth in the *Caloil* decision does not go the full distance. Major questions basic to the effective resolution of the critical marketing issues of today remain unanswered.

For example, what is to be done where a producing province is unwilling to develop an indigenous resource in favour of an extraprovincial consumer? What happens in those cases where a producing province reserves a higher percentage of its producing oil or gas at the expense of dependent consumers in other provinces, as may well occur in the not too distant future in the case of Alberta's production? And what can be done where a province does not wish to provide a bridge for the movement of energy resources from one province to others, or to the U.S. export market, as is now the case with respect to the Quebec and Labrador controversy concerning the proposed transmission of Labrador power to the U.S. northeast states?

In all of these cases, more central control is an elementary step towards effective achievement of a higher degree of supply security and some control over energy cost structures in the national energy market. If a single province can with impunity unilaterally refuse to transmit power or energy resources from an adjacent province, or is able unilaterally to reduce production of an indigenous resource to the (deliberate?) jeopardy of Canadian consumers in other provinces, then the basic issues of price and supply will forever lie outside national control. Indeed, the sheer magnitude of Canada's stake in maintaining at least some control over these issues may in turn lean inescapably in favour of the constitutional power to regulate on a general theory of the trade and commerce power.

The so-called "general trade and commerce power" applies wherever there are issues of such fundamental importance to the national economy as to warrant federal intervention, notwithstanding the technical question of whether there exist extraprovincial trade flows. In the particular context of energy marketing, the general power would tend to support federal legislative measures that go beyond the strict regulation of already established interprovincial and international trade movements, to include possibly a measure of control over intraprovincial energy production in much the same way as today applies to wheat production and marketing.

In a strict sense, the limits placed upon the general theory are not readily ascertainable. A Supreme Court decision in 1976 appeared to suggest that this view of the trade and commerce power could support almost any federal "regulatory scheme." In the *Anti-Inflation Reference*, which was also heard in 1976, the Chief Justice indicated that he would have been receptive to a trade and commerce argument had one been advanced. He went on to say that:

> . . .the *Anti-Inflation Act* is not directed to any particular trade. It is

105

directed to suppliers of commodities and services in general and to the public services of governments, and to the relationship of these suppliers and of the public services to those employed by and in them, and to their overall relationship to the public. With respect to some of such suppliers and with respect to the federal public service, federal legislative power needs no support from the existence of exceptional circumstances to justify the introduction of a policy of restraint to combat inflation.[15]

In short, the exact extent of the support available under the general theory must await judicial detailing. But, the details notwithstanding, a federal regulatory scheme created to resolve issues basic to the welfare of the economy at large can find some justification under trade and commerce as generally applied.

As a necessary corollary to the rejuvenation of the trade and commerce power, the strictures upon provincial regulatory control over intraprovincial transactions that involve markets which are ultimately national are now quite substantial. For example, there is now settled law which makes ineffective any provincial legislation which purports to regulate imports to aid the operation of a local marketing scheme.[16] Such provincial controls that do affect interprovincial trade may only be defended if they are (a) incidental, (b) unavoidable and (c) part of a plan which in pith and substance lies clearly within provincial competence.[17] While the relevant cases here define provincial power by inference, they also suggest a very substantially widened basis for federal market regulation under trade and commerce.

Peace, Order and Good Government
The trade and commerce power is not the sole constitutional basis for a federal marketing board along the lines discussed in this study. The federal government's jurisdiction under "Peace, Order and Good Government" (POGG) would appear also to apply.

A major purpose of POGG is to allow lacunae or gaps within the present distribution of powers between the federal and provincial governments to be filled. Whenever legislation can be said to involve a "matter" or a purpose which is in "pith and substance" not included within any of the enumerated heads of sections 91 and 92 of the British North America Act, then it can be the subject of the central government's residuary jurisdiction. In this regard, semantics play an often critical, if not decisive, role in the determination of which level of government ultimately has constitutional power.

. . .the issue with respect to the general power . . . is to determine what are to be considered to be single, indivisible matters of national interest and concern lying outside the specific heads of jurisdiction in sections 91 and 92. It is possible to invent such matters by applying new names to old legislative purposes. There is an increasing tendency to sum up a wide variety of legislative purposes in single, comprehensive designations. Control of inflation, environmental protection, and preservation of the national identity or independence are examples.

Many matters within provincial jurisdiction can be transformed by being treated as part of a larger subject or concept for which no place can be found within that jurisdiction. This perspective has a close affinity to the notion that there must be a single, plenary power to deal effectively and completely with any problem. The future of the general power, in the absence of emergency, will depend very much on the approach that the courts adopt to this issue of characterization.[18]

While the application of POGG as a means of plugging holes in the constitutional fabric has been the subject of some debate in individual cases, its validity in principle in respect of this function has rarely been challenged. There is, however, much argument with respect to its other employments: namely, in answer to regulatory issues having a "national dimension" or as a means of coping with state "emergencies."

The so-called "national dimensions test" was first propounded in an 1882 Privy Council decision, *Russell* v. *The Queen*.[19] It was suggested that whenever Parliament considered a problem to be "one of general concern to the Dominion upon which uniformity of legislation is desirable," then it could assume the power to legislate under POGG. The apparent scope of jurisdiction allowed the central government under this test was nothing less than awesome. Indeed, in a subsequent decision the Privy Council felt moved to suggest that the wide power it had described in *Russell* was one that required "great care."[20]

Despite this early support for central regulatory authority, the trend of judicial decision-making took a sharp, sudden and completely unexpected turn for the worse during the tenure of what some constitutional text writers fondly refer to as the "wicked stepfathers of Confederation," Viscount Haldane and Lord Watson. Haldane, in particular, held firmly to the view that POGG conceived of extraordinary powers which could apply only to extraordinary circumstances. The presence or absence of an emergency totally eclipsed the national dimensions test as the critical issue to constitutional validity during this era.

The national dimensions test remained moribund until 1932 when a reference was made, in passing, to some aspects of aviation of national significance to the "body politic of the Dominion" (e.g., navigation and national commitments under an international treaty). It was a deceptively significant reference. Because the Privy Council had viewed POGG as valid only in the context of emergencies, it had virtually condemned all relevant federal legislation to a finite lifetime (given emergencies to be by definition temporary).[21] Now for the first time there was a reference again to circumstances where legislation of a permanent character would be appropriate under POGG.

A clearer resurrection of the general power of POGG occurred in 1946 when the Privy Council contended that:

> . . . the true test must be found in the real subject matter of the legislation: if it is such that it goes beyond local or provincial concern or interests and must from its inherent nature be the concern of the Dominion as a whole (as, for example in the *Aeronautics* case and the *Radio* case), then it will fall within the competence of the Dominion Parliament as a matter affecting the peace, order and good government of Canada, although it may in another aspect touch on matters specially reserved to the provincial legislatures. War and pestilence, no doubt, are instances; so too, may be the drink or drug traffic, or the carrying of arms. In *Russell* v. *The Queen*, Sir Montague Smith gave as an instance of valid Dominion legislation a law which prohibited or restricted the sale or exposure of cattle having a contagious disease. Nor is the validity of the legislation, when due to its inherent nature, affected because there may still be room for enactments by a provincial legislature dealing with an aspect of the same subject in so far as it specifically affects that province.[22]

This decision set forth the so-called "Canada Temperance test" which in actual fact was little more than a reincarnation of the national dimensions test, only by another name. Unlike its predecessor, the principle of the Canada Temperance decision has been cited approvingly in almost all of the major POGG cases that have been heard since 1949.

But while the Canada Temperance decision re-established the legitimacy of general legislation under POGG, it was left for later cases to add the necessary specifics. A coherent set of guidelines remains problematic, and the proper scope of the general power under POGG continues to be the subject of some speculation. Some constitutional writers believe that the national dimensions concept was originally based upon a geographic principle and applied only in those situations where the need for legislative uniformity could be satisfied only through a federal enactment. According to this view, whenever a failure of one or more provinces to act would have serious consequences for residents of other provinces, then the national dimensions test would clearly apply and the federal government would be free to act as a result.[23]

Another imaginative interpretation[24] centres upon a reconciliation between the emergency and Canada Temperance theories. Here an effort is made to divide legislative subject areas into "naturally unified" categories (e.g., aviation, or the National Capital Commission) as opposed to less specific and potentially all-inclusive subjects (e.g., environmental pollution, linguistic rights, or wage and price controls). While the first category of subject matter might involve an apparent displacement of provincial legislative jurisdiction, the effect is confined to the limited requirements of the thing being regulated. To take power over airlines would allow the federal government only limited jurisdiction with respect to commercial transactions completed in the provinces relevant to this one industry. On the other hand, wage and price controls afford a much wider sweep over commercial dealings of virtually all types, and might, if permanently put in place by the federal government, do enormous violence to the distribution of powers contemplated under sections 91 and 92 of the constitution. Because wage and price control involves a potentially unlimited sphere of jurisdiction, Ottawa would, according to this view, temporarily assume regulatory power, and at that, only when motivated by the existence of emergency conditions such as prolonged double-digit inflation.[25]

The Present Provincial Position
Since the halcyon days of the Privy Council under Viscount Haldane, the scope of jurisdiction available to Parliament under the trade and commerce power and POGG has vastly increased. Both now offer ample foundation for the implementation of a comprehensive energy marketing scheme along the lines described in this study. But the precise reach of federal jurisdiction back to the source of production remains a highly contentious issue so far as petroleum and natural gas are concerned.

Simply stated, the producing provinces claim a power to regulate Crown-owned petroleum and gas that is uniquely anchored. In the particular case of Alberta, it is argued that the Resources Transfer Act was the result of an effort by Parliament to put the province on an equal footing with the original parties to Confederation so far as Crown or provincial resource ownership was concerned. As a result, according to this interpretation, the relevant terms of the BNA Act are now as applicable to Alberta as they have been to Nova Scotia and Prince

Edward Island. Sections 109 and 92(5) are the particular provisions of interest here.[26] At first blush, they appear to lend a certain credence to the Alberta claim. Provincial proprietary and legislative power over public land is apparently defined to exclude, under normal circumstances, the possibility of pre-emptory legislation by Parliament. But there are nonetheless some fine points that create uncertainty. For example, can oil and gas in situ be properly termed "land" and therefore part of the provincial Crown proprietary interest as specified under section 95(5), as against being simply a commodity or chattel (which oil and gas clearly become at the point of production)? Should this issue be resolved affirmatively, oil and gas in situ would not then technically be "in a stream of commerce" and, prior to production, would apparently remain beyond the reach of Parliament under the trade and commerce power.

As of mid 1982, the Alberta position had been the subject of at least one carefully structured judicial test. The province successfully contended before the provincial Court of Appeal that the federal tax on natural gas was ultra vires to the extent that it involved provincially-owned production from Crown reserves. While this decision should probably be appealed, in the meantime there continues to be a measure of doubt as to whether federal legislation can properly reach back to regulate productions from reserves that are within the public lands of the province.

But even assuming the possibly unlikely event of a Supreme Court of Canada decision that agrees with the Alberta view, the long-term effects are unclear. Presumably the province may consider a massive expropriation of all Crown leases, with the private producers concerned being put under service contracts. In this way, the province would be put in the best possible constitutional position with respect to the regulation of its petroleum and gas. But in practical terms how much would this really accomplish in marketing control?

Alberta, in taking this step, would acquire no more than the power to threaten to withhold a significant proportion, if not indeed the entirety, of its production. But it is very unlikely that the province would as a result be able to pick and choose between individual buyers beyond the limits of the province. Trade beyond provincial borders would still lie within Ottawa's jurisdiction, as would the power to regulate the all-important matter of price in interprovincial and international markets. Alberta would as a result be driven to stopping production only when the proposed price was unacceptable. But even in this extreme case, there are large legal and even larger practical "ifs" involved. Ottawa, like Alberta, retains considerable practical and certain legal retaliatory power in the event of a stand-off of these proportions. It could restrict or even deny Alberta access to any or all markets outside of the province. Such a deliberately prejudicial and discriminatory step may well be unthinkable, but as a legal fact it is clear that Alberta does not alone possess all the bargaining leverage.

Ottawa also has available wide emergency powers under the residuary clause, which would undoubtedly provide enough room to force Alberta to produce should the effects of restrained production be sufficiently serious in terms of Canada's overall economic performance. As a practical issue, there is no serious doubt that a prolonged production embargo would generate emergency conditions sufficient to attract the attention of Parliament. Should legislation be the result, the provincial claims to jurisdiction under sections 101 and 95(5) of the constitution would have little more than theoretical content.

The Federal Declaratory Power
Under section 92(10)(c) of the BNA Act, the federal government has a decisive weapon in the event of an irreconcilable deadlock in its negotiations with any of the producing provinces. This is the so-called ''declaratory power'' which allows Parliament the unilateral power to declare specific works (and undertakings) to be within federal jurisdiction, notwithstanding the presence of either valid provincial regulatory jurisdiction or even provincial ownership. But, despite the apparently broad scope of power under section 92(10)(c), there are a number of significant practical and legal limitations that bear notice.

First, the declaratory power applies only in respect of specific works and undertakings. Unlike Parliament's jurisdiction under POGG, section 92(10)(c) provides no general regulatory power with respect to classes of subjects beyond the individual items specified in the declaration itself. Thus, to obtain regulatory control over oil wells or power dams otherwise under provincial jurisdiction, the specific wells and dams in question would have to be described in unequivocably clear terms to be brought within the purview of the declaration.

Second, the impact of a declaration does not involve any transfer of proprietary interest as would result from an expropriation. The declaration will only transfer regulatory authority, leaving the original ownership interest undisturbed.

Third, as a practical matter, the declaratory power has become increasingly regarded as being exceptional, and it is unlikely to be brought into play except under the most extreme circumstances. It is technically available, however, and there is some history of its employment as a means of overcoming otherwise irreconcilable obstacles to federal legislation in the national interest. The creation of a comprehensive national regulatory mechanism to control wheat production and marketing ultimately had to depend upon the declaratory power.

In the case of oil and gas producing facilities otherwise liable to provincial regulation, there is no a priori legal obstacle preventing resort to the federal declaratory power. But there are very real concerns with regard to the scope of power Ottawa might acquire as a result. It is highly improbable that any more than the power to regulate the physical facilities would be secured. Oil and gas in situ would continue to be under provincial power so far as Crown reserves were concerned. For this reason the province would in theory retain the legal option to restrain or halt production at any time.

On the other hand, the declaratory power could be employed to restrict provincial legislation to the production-conservation function, leaving the federal government with the power over all marketing decisions at both the intra- and extraprovincial levels. In this fashion, the likelihood of any of the producing provinces in future attempting to reserve a higher percentage for indigenous markets could be avoided.

At a political level, appealing to this extraordinary constitutional tool would undoubtedly emphasize the unwillingness of the federal government to tolerate fundamental stand-offs over resource issues that prejudiced the economic lifeblood of the country. To this extent, the provincial governments would be offered a timely, albeit highly controversial, reminder of the primary jurisdictional servitude of the central government to the best interest of the country as a whole.

State Intervention: Alternatives

Overall, the federal government can fall back upon a wide range of constitutional powers should a major stand-off with the producing provinces develop again. The present constitutional framework would seem technically to allow Ottawa to implement comprehensive regulatory controls which, in the absence of an emergency, would likely fall short of allowing Ottawa to force production from provincial Crown reserves, but would nonetheless permit wide de facto control over all production from all sources. Despite the fact that recent trends of constitutional interpretation have widened the scope for central legislative action, and while the recent changes to Canada's energy picture over the course of the decade suggest the wisdom of more central action, federal-provincial relations have moved in an opposite direction. Indeed, it has been suggested that the sweeping powers of intervention described are all but politically moribund in light of both contemporary provincial expectations and the discussions of fundamental constitutional change.

As an issue of philosophy and practicality, Canada's energy difficulties have become complex to a degree that far outstrips the capacities of eleven independent governments with eleven often conflicting legislative and political agendas. The current alienation of the oil-producing provinces of the West, the lowered marginal investment expectations of the energy sector generally, widespread confusion about the nation's energy prospects, and the maintenance of a thoroughly jumbled, and at times irrational, fiscal and tax expenditure system, are all factors that cry for a rational policy for the country as a whole.

As discussed in chapter 2, the National Energy Program was a major first step towards the implementation of a comprehensive national energy management scheme. The NEP came forward at a time when conventional oil and gas prospects had set into decline, and new initiatives where essential. This, plus the NEP's special incentives favouring Canada lands, has ensured that remaining provincial conventional prospects will receive less future attention. All else being equal, the provincial share of export sales will likely decline as production from federally-controlled lands increases. For this reason, there exists a very large incentive for the producing provinces to re-examine the importance of establishing a systematic national marketing system, if only to preserve a share of export revenue through an equitable allocation of markets between federal and provincial sources of production.

Canada might also take stock of mechanisms through which the growing gap between the lowest-cost conventional sources of oil and gas and the high-cost supplies of the frontier might be effectively brought under control. Energy price regulation will have to take into account many factors, including domestic and export sales, variations within the domestic market, and the degree to which various sources of energy might be "rolled" together to produce an effective pricing mechanism nationwide.

A recurrent theme in the preceding discussion has been the contention that Canada's energy problems are more the product of regulatory deficiencies than any other single factor. It is now necessary to address directly the need for comprehensive controls over energy pricing and marketing in Canada which, if unattended, may delay development of needed new supplies.

Inevitably, the role that can be played through increased direct state participation will be considered. There are ample precedents both within Canada and abroad that forcefully establish the importance of the role that can be played by state energy corporations. But both history and contemporary experience suggest that too great a burden should not be placed upon Crown corporations as primary vehicles for contending with complex regulatory problems which deserve direct legislative effort.

In many countries state involvement in at least the oil and gas industry has been the result of protracted government-industry disputes over revenues. One or a combination of three situations usually has been the final outcome:

- state monopolies over all phases of oil and gas production and (domestic) marketing;
- imposition of strict production-sharing contracts with equity in the oil and gas itself retained by the state;
- establishment of work conditions stipulating local procurement and employment obligations.

A number of different examples are briefly discussed in the paragraphs that follow. Further examples are given in the Appendix.

Japan
The Japanese regulatory structure was a response to a long history of fear concerning foreign domination of the domestic economy, the need to develop and distribute as much of the benefits of local economic activity as possible amongst a large population, and, perhaps most fundamentally, an overwhelming scarcity of indigenous energy resources. The main contemporary regulatory objects include (a) satisfaction of the domestic economic need for more energy, and (b) increasing the level of control enjoyed by Japan over import sources of supply.

Japan has been far less concerned than most Western countries over the philosophic issue of the appropriate balance between private versus public enterprise. A succession of Japanese governments established, and today maintains, a highly coordinated supportive approach to business activity. Thus the JPDC (Japanese Petroleum Development Corporation) and MITI (Ministry of International Trade and Industry), to take two examples, both exist to support Japanese business activity on the simple premise that a build-up of Japanese capital will be more

114

likely to benefit the domestic economy and the welfare of the Japanese people than would involvement by a foreign operator.

The Japanese petroleum industry is regulated by MITI, which was given authority in 1962 to grant licences and permits for construction and expansion of refineries, to control levels of operations, and to control import prices by regulation of the refiners' plants. MITI established the Agency for Natural Resources and Energy (ANRE), having jurisdiction over energy policies, including review of foreign investment applications. ANRE was to implement the national energy policy.

MITI attempted to increase the share of the domestic market given to Japanese oil companies by providing low-interest loans and preferential treatment with respect to refinery applications and service station allocations. Exploration abroad was similarly encouraged. In 1967 the JPDC was established with public funding to stimulate Japanese development of overseas exploration and development. In 1978, the JPDC was used to negotiate with the People's Republic of China with respect to a contract to develop crude production in the Gulf of Chihli. Both the JPDC and private oil companies are involved in the proposed development. Japanese imports of liquified natural gas from Alaska, Brunei, Abu Dhabi and Indonesia were negotiated primarily by the JPDC on behalf of several groups of both Japanese and international oil companies. Most of the exploration and importing of oil is carried on by private oil companies. The JPDC appears to be used for its diplomatic services and to ensure that as much of the market as possible is served by Japanese companies.

The Japanese example offers important lessons for Canada in terms of the development of policies that can enhance Canadian trading opportunities and the potential productivity of government-business cooperation in export development. But from the particular standpoint of the role of a state energy corporation, the case of Japan, while generally instructive, is somewhat unique on its own facts. Japan lacks indigenous resources where Canada appears to have enormous potential. Japan's economy is not dominated by foreign investment while Canada's is. Japan's growth has been dominated by secondary processing and manufacturing activity, while Canada's economy continues to be ruled by primary and extractive activity. And, finally, Japan is a geographic island with a distinct culture and a long history of independence, whereas Canada shares the longest undefended border in the world with one of the most heavily-industrialized powers on earth. The Canadian and American relationship involves difficult and complex interdependencies which must be considered.

Norway

The Norwegian oil policy has been formulated by the Oil and Minerals Division of the Ministry of Industry. The jurisdiction of this ministry includes the planning, administration and regulation of technical and economic affairs of the oil and gas industry, as well as directing negotiations with specific oil companies on the government's behalf. Prior to 1969 licences were granted to develop oil and gas without any state participation requirements. In that year, the licences were amended to include a state "carried" or "net profit" interest. This carried interest provided Norway with the option of participating directly in the exploitation of commercial discoveries. It gave the state a portion of profits of any find that was developed by private concerns in all cases.

In 1972, Statoil was established as a holding company for the government's interest in exploration licences. Shortly afterwards new legislation was enacted to increase royalties and ensure Statoil's right of participation in all exploration without obligation to bear any of the initial costs. Licences granted between 1974 and 1976 include Statoil as a mandatory participant without exploration cost obligations. The company, however, does have obligations with respect to development costs. It is entitled to receive 50 to 55 per cent of any profits, increasing to a share of 66 to 75 per cent depending upon the maximum level of production actually achieved. Statoil takes some of the oil and gas that is paid to the government as part of the government's royalties. The gas is exported through a pipeline to Emden, West Germany. The oil is sold by Statoil to another state company, Norsk Olje. Refining takes place in the town of Mongstad, where there is a facility which is itself a 60-40 state-private venture.

The Norwegian state oil company is also involved in petrochemical production. It holds a 33 per cent interest in a joint venture called Noretyl, which operates a 300,000 tonne per year ethylene plant. The same group also owns a 100,000 tonne per year low-density polyethylene plant and a 500,000 tonne per year polypropylene plant in Bramble which came on-stream in 1978.

The Norwegian experience reflects a highly coordinated effort to secure a maximum amount of benefit for the local economy through a meshing of state enterprise and concession regulation. While Statoil's finances have been under pressure as a result of heavy production investments, and despite significant impending over-capacity problems within the support sectors, the Norwegian approach has been highly successfuly in securing large gains for the country.

116

France

The French government has played a major role in the petroleum industry since 1928 when a government monopoly was established to control all imports into the country. The government supervises the industry through French oil companies whose authorization is subject to periodical review and revision by government. There are three types of companies today in France: those that are completely state owned, those that enjoy mixed public and private equity, and those that are wholly private but hold licences through the government. Exploration in France cannot take place without government licences. When discoveries are made, production approval is in the form of either a 50-year concession in the case of major discoveries, or a production permit renewable for three 5-year periods where a small deposit is in issue. Exports of domestically produced oil are subject to government approval.

In 1966, government-sponsored oil companies were consolidated under a major state-owned oil company, ERAP (Entreprise de Recherches et d'Activités Pétrolières). ERAP was given advantages in the market, including being designated sole supplier to selective state enterprises such as Air France and the newly-nationalized railroads. It was also given long-term interest-free loans, and had a 25 per cent share of the national market reserved for its product. The largest mixed private and public company is CFP (Compagnie Française des Pétroles) which is 35 per cent state owned. It was established in 1924.

While French companies participate in overseas exploration and development, much of France's petroleum industry is concentrated in the refining sectors. Government control of the refining industry is exercised through laws that require all refineries, regardless of their ownership, to utilize specified quantities of crude supplied by French companies. A government conservation agency (Agence pour les Economies d'Energie) was established in 1976 and set import ceilings to further these policies. However, in doing so the government contravened European Economic Community regulations, and in 1978 the 50 per cent market reservation for French refineries was liberalized. In 1974 and again in 1980 the French government bypassed the private companies altogether in negotiating government-to-government contracts for oil imports from Iraq and Saudia Arabia.

French exploration interests have been active in the Middle East, Africa, Canada, United States, Australia, and in the North Sea. In 1980 a five-year plan was launched to increase domestic exploration through improved technology whereby high-risk and previously

117

inaccessible zones might be exploited. The success of this effort has been mixed.

French gas production and distribution is regulated by Gaz de France, also a state-owned company. This company has entered into contracts to import gas from the Soviet Union and the Netherlands. It is also involved in a 20-year contract to import liquified natural gas (LNG) from Algeria.

France has, in summary, shown a consistently result-oriented approach in its management of the oil and gas industry. It has been prepared to adopt whatever measures necessary to secure French interests, including nationalization, creation of market monopolies, and the imposition of import quotas to the advantage of French corporations.

Italy

Italy's earliest state interest in the petroleum industry was established through AGIP (Axienda Generale Italiana Petroli), a private company which was to explore for petroleum in Italy using state funds. Very little success was achieved. AGIP later became part of ENI (Ente Nazionale Idrocarburi) which was established in 1953. ENI was completely state owned and was to be the holding company for Italy's oil interest. In 1969 the company became the leading exploration, production, and refining operator in Italy when it purchased Royal Dutch Shell's Italian subsidiary along with its refineries and all of its service stations. ENI continues to explore within Italy and has had some recent successes. Much of Italy's enormous refinery industry, however, continues to be foreign owned.

Italian participation in exploration in foreign countries is largely through ENI. In 1977, ENI entered into exploration contracts with Brazil, South Yemen, and Vietnam. ENI is also involved through AGIP in exploration off shore in Iran, Qatar, the Congo and Norway, and on shore in Nigeria, Tunisia, Libya and Egypt.

ENI assumed responsibility for Italian gas exploration and production when it was first formed in 1953. As domestic Italian needs grew, ENI entered into import contracts with Tunisia, Algeria, the Netherlands and the USSR. ENI, in addition has arrangements to import LNG from Libya. Algeria and Tunisia have both contracted with the state corporation to build a gas pipeline from Algeria across the Mediterranean to Sicily. ENI also has responsibility for all uranium exploration and development. Through a subsidiary, AGIP Nucleare, it holds exploration interests in the U.S., Canada, Australia, Zambia, Bolivia and Nigeria, and is actively searching for uranium deposits.

Italian experience, like that of France, has been more goal-directed than the product of a coherent philosophy about the role of the state. Nevertheless, the government has a very large and effective state presence which is protected through selective market monopolies and fiscal support.

Indonesia
In 1963, Indonesia passed legislation prohibiting foreign companies from having concession rights to exploit Indonesian resources. From this point on, production was only permitted on a ''contract-of-work'' basis with the then domestic oil companies, Pertamin, Permina and Permigan.

In 1968, these three companies were merged to form Pertamina, a single state-owned monopoly. Pertamina's charter was revised to give it responsibility over the oil and gas industry in Indonesia in its totality. Today the company supervises operations of all foreign interests involved in petroleum exploration, production and distribution. All refineries in the country are owned and operated by the state, as are all domestic distribution facilities. Pertamina enjoyed extensive autonomy until 1975 when, following its near financial collapse, the government began to exercise stricter control through the Ministry of Mining, which today has formal supervisory jurisdiction over the company.

Pertamina is a major source of public revenues for Indonesia. These are shared with the government according to the following percentages:

• 60 per cent of net operating income from its own operations,
• 50 per cent of income received through production-sharing agreements, and
• all revenues from contract-of-work agreements.

Contract-of-work agreements with major foreign oil companies require the foreign operators to supply exploration and development funds, expertise in technical and managerial areas, and training programs for Indonesian workers. When production has begun, the contracting company provides oil to Pertamina at cost plus 20 cents per barrel and up to 20 per cent of oil produced at export prices. It must also split revenue on a 60/40 ratio in Pertamina's favour. The contractor receives oil to cover costs and depreciation. Roughly half of Indonesia's crude oil is produced on this basis.

Production-sharing agreements account for an additional 45 per cent of production. These agreements provide Pertamina with management control and split the exploration costs equally. The profit division is in terms of oil rather than profits, with the ratios varying from 85/15 to 89/11 in Pertamina's favour.

Both kinds of agreements vest ownership in all equipment brought into Indonesia in Pertamina. Equipment is leased back to the oil companies concerned.

In 1976 all existing contracts were renegotiated to finance Pertamina's debt. Profits to the foreign oil companies were lowered, and the period of time over which companies' costs could be recovered was increased. New contracts were devised for high-risk areas, increasing the profit split in favour of the companies to 14 to 15 per cent in the event of a commercial discovery. Pertamina and Mobil entered into a profit-sharing agreement in 1978 and began producing liquid natural gas from the Arun field for export to Japan and the United States. In 1979, Pertamina began plans for an ethylene facility in North Sumatra and was seeking a partner for this as a joint venture.

The Indonesian experience is in most respects peculiar in its own facts. But the Pertamina case is nevertheless instructive for any inquiry into the strengths and weaknesses of massive state monopoly control over the oil and gas industry as a means of serving public policy objectives. Throughout their history, Pertamina's antecedent companies were repeatedly called upon to assume responsibility over the full spectrum of oil and gas operations and address, successfully, each new need as it arose. In time, the companies had an impossible diversity of enterprises under their charge, including hospitals, communications systems, and even a chain of hotels. In each case there was ample initial justification in support of these activities. Hospitals and schools, for example, were developed in order to entice foreign oil and gas expertise. Communication services resulted from the effort to overcome the deficiencies of the civilian system and establish a more reliable alternative for company operations. But these enterprises taxed the already sizeable managerial load upon Pertamina and eroded its internal commercial discipline. Events moved from bad to worse until 1976 when a major effort was needed to avoid financial collapse of the company. Subsequently many of the non-energy-related subsidiaries were spun off, and Pertamina's finances were brought more or less under control.

Conclusions
If generalizations are possible at all, the Pertamina experience illustrates, in exaggerated fashion, that more than a statutory monopoly

is usually required to serve the national interest. Pertamina, like all state ventures, had to face constraints distinct from those facing the government that created it. It ultimately could not escape the need to conform to the fundamental commercial imperatives of the international marketplace. Since its inception, Pertamina has often relied upon joint venture operations, and has always had to depend upon foreign expertise both to realize facilities and to manage many of its operations. Pertamina is nonetheless a fully-integrated operation involving every phase of the oil and gas industry from exploration to marketing. It thus offers some useful lessons vis-à-vis comprehensive state entries into the industry which, in light of Canada's NEP, promise to be every bit as all-encompassing, albeit less pre-emptory of private investment.

There are, however, limitations of immediate note in drawing out any Indonesian-Canadian comparisons. Canada's oil and gas industry has been structured around a large domestic market with historically large growth prospects. To this degree the industry is more permanently rooted in the local economy than is true of many producing nations which lack large indigenous oil- and gas-consuming industries, or materially-expectant populations. Indonesia has the sheer weight of population, but it remains one of the poorest nations on earth and has demonstrated enough political instability to cause concern for prospective investors. As a result, foreign capital has concentrated in production, and domestic Indonesian refining and market development has received little attention.

A fully-integrated oil and gas industry has developed in Canada, with the domestic economy building up a substantial secondary infrastructure in the refining and petrochemical sectors. This has in turn ensured a capturing of secondary industrial advantages from oil and gas production. For most of the producing world, localizing these significant economic spin-offs has been difficult, if not impossible. For Indonesia, the acquisition of a substantial domestic processing base continues to be something of an uphill effort.

For Canada, by virtue of its general economic development, the discovery of commercial quantities of petroleum and natural gas has ensured secondary development far beyond what has proven true for most of the producing world. Perhaps for the same reason, Canada's manner in dealing with the industry has been fundamentally out of step with most of the petroleum-dependent world. Industry reinvestment in the domestic economy has been simply assumed, and Canada's willingness to provide substantial tax and fiscal concessions to a

121

foreign-dominated economic sector has continued without much public scrutiny of the amount of benefits in fact being received.

Canada's continued status as a world producer is now in some doubt, and there is concern that industry activity be maintained at a brisk pace. A re-examination of the overall political and legislative controls over the industry and the appropriate level of direct involvement has begun, as evidenced by the National Energy Program. But as state companies such as Pertamina, Statoil, ENI and others clearly establish, mere creation of a higher national presence will not of itself guarantee retention of the economic rent associated with oil and gas production. Without a national monopoly or unlimited public funding, the state corporation must respond to the commercial restraints of the market within which it exists. In Canada's case, the industry environment is highly commercial, being dominated by private multinationals which account for the bulk of domestic production and, in a book sense, the lion's share of reinvestment. As a competitor, and at times joint venture partner, private firms still impose pressure to adhere to highly cost-competitive standards in corporate decision-making, statutory mandate or no statutory mandate.

For state corporations like Petro-Canada, Statoil or ENI, a series of difficult choices are inevitable. All are creatures of statute and thereby obliged to the legislative priorities that caused their creation in the first instance. Often the force of both public necessity and law compel decisions decidedly outside of the immediate dictates of short-run commercial prudence, such as the early (and effective) supporting activity in what seemed at times a commercially barren region. But equally there is constant external and internal pressure to conform to the dictates of short-term commercial reality, and as often as not, private partnership agreements will compel adherence to short-run commercial prudence. Moreover, at a less formal but undoubtedly influential level, pressure is exerted upon state companies by both public and industry to show high standards of cost effectiveness. This, plus the effort to maintain an internal sense of commercial discipline, usually produces a cost consciousness above that which might be expected of situationally-unique Crown corporations such as the National Capital Commission or the National Arts Centre.

The oil and gas industry has a fundamental commercial orientation that has an equally fundamental influence over the entire spectrum of companies — public, private, and state corporation alike — that comprise the whole. But simultaneous service of a public mandate and adherence to the dictates of commercial reality are next to a definitional impossibility. To the extent that a default on one side or the other is more or less guaranteed, a state corporation in competition with private companies will be the subject of constant criticism, if not some skepticism.

By contrast, a state monopoly such as Pertamina can enjoy a tremendous (although not unlimited) advantage. Being in a monopoly position by definition does away with an immediate commercial standard, although financial performance comparisons will still be made at an international level and on a sector rate of return basis. As the 1975-76 financial plight of Pertamina demonstrated, state monopoly status does not give an immunity from the international financial community upon which all major state oil and gas corporations are to some degree dependent.

In Canada's case, the private oil and gas sector enjoys a vitality and drive which is as important to the realization of future production ambitions as it is difficult to quantify. Displacement of private activity in the name of a state monopoly would not, in the writer's view, be justifiable at this time. Such a step should be a decidedly twelfth-hour option. The country's energy problems can and perhaps should first be subjected to more effective regulatory controls that will better accommodate the national interest. Today there are a series of major policy bottlenecks that could not be resolved by simply increasing the public's equity in the industry. They include:

- establishing and maintaining an effective pricing system with provincial consent;
- developing a mechanism through which frontier and synthetic prices can be blended into a uniform domestic price;
- developing and maintaining a comprehensive cost data base on an all-sources supply basis;
- developing and maintaining a higher level of market information with respect to price elasticity effects, the economic impact of price restructuring, degree of substitution obtainable, etc.;
- establishing a market allocation method (export and domestic) to ensure a reasonable balance between Canada lands production and provincial sources;
- establishing a land banking system that can ensure management of Crown reserves;
- establishing a system to encourage highest-value applications for finite oil and gas resources;
- resolving jurisdictional issues over Canada lands.

In all the above cases, it would be unrealistic to assume that more state equity or higher Canadian ownership would be an effective remedy. Each issue involves long-term policy matters and, in several cases, intergovernmental complexities that condemn the utility of anything less than direct regulatory intervention.

Market Regulation

This analysis has attempted to show that more than the existing controls will be needed to contend with the difficult energy problems that Canadians will face during the balance of this century. Establishment of a National Energy Marketing Board with initial jurisdiction to improve, detail and recommend comprehensive and durable solutions to the federal government would be, in this context, a useful first step.

Marketing boards have been the subject of considerable debate. That they represent an extreme intervention in the affairs of the private market is beyond doubt. The issue of substance, however, is the case that might be made for their possible use, all issues of general ideology momentarily aside. In this regard, three factors appear to be relevant. First, will a marketing board assist in the orderly development and servicing of actual or potential markets which otherwise might be less reliably satisfied? Second, will the creation of a marketing board help to generate an investment climate conducive to realizing the desirable level of domestic productive capacity in a manner that is demonstrably superior to that of the unregulated market? And third, is the industry that is being controlled through a marketing mechanism of sufficient importance to warrant the effort and expense involved in governmental regulation?

The importance of energy to the national economy need not be further emphasized. The remaining two issues concerning market service and industry investment also appear to raise little real controversy. In some areas, most notably petroleum, production has fallen off and projected market needs are in danger of being unmet. Some respected authorities have described a future of increasingly difficult supply problems necessitating painful market adjustments. On the industry investment side, the level of direct and indirect public financial support is today at such an advanced state as to leave no room for debate as to the fact, let alone the need, of state involvement.

Canada's prior experience has been confined primarily to agricultural marketing boards. Notably, this device has most often been used in an attempt to support regulated prices to improve farmer incomes, rather than to allocate short supplies equitably among consumers. But, this difference notwithstanding, most of the agricultural plans in force are designed to benefit both producers and the public at large, and therefore deserve mention as examples of efforts by government to control the marketing of certain essential products for the good of the economy as a whole.

There are currently in excess of one hundred agricultural marketing boards in Canada that have responsibility over products ranging from pulpwood to eggs. As one might expect with such a proliferation, their powers vary widely, with responsibilities ranging between pure research and promotion funded through compulsory producer levies, to virtual domination over all market functions, including volume of sales and pricing. Indeed, in 1978 more than 75 per cent of Canadian farm output was subject to some form of regulated control.

As described above, the constitutional history of farm product marketing has been complex, with the ultimate effect being a heavy (although far from exclusive) emphasis today upon federal-provincial cooperation as opposed to the unilateral imposition of central regulatory schemes. An example of a wholly-centralized scheme, however, can be found in the Canada Wheat Board which is, by virtue of section 4(4) of the Canadian Wheat Board Act, bound to ensure the orderly marketing of grain in interprovincial and international markets. Its powers in pursuit of this broad objective are extensive, including the purchasing, taking delivery, storing, transferring, selling, shipping or otherwise disposing of grain. The board can contract and make credit arrangements in its own right, operate elevators as needed, as well as create or make use of whatever marketing facilities it thinks necessary for its effective operation. It can (and does) set selling prices, with profits going towards the Consolidated Revenue Fund, unless invested by the board under its statutory power.

Quite apart from its other functions, the Wheat Board operates through a quota system which limits a farmer's right to deliver to an elevator or a freight car (i.e., the national market) according to the particular terms of his permit book which stipulates both location and the quantity that he can sell. This quota cannot be exceeded. The board in short has assumed the role of exclusive buyer or monopsonist, paying a price set by cabinet and based upon Number 1 Manitoba Northern Wheat as the standard. The administration costs of the board are charged directly against sale revenues prior to the distribution to the producers.

The strength of the Wheat Board lies in the federal jurisdiction over all extraprovincial markets, and the placing of all such transactions firmly under the board's control by ensuring that all wheat moving between provinces or into export is owned by the board itself. Market pricing is understandably the most critical issue because of its controlling bearing upon producer revenues. In this connection, it is of more than passing interest that since 1973 the board has followed the practice of two-tier pricing, under which domestic consumers are protected from the occasionally higher international price standards.

The involvement of the board pricing policies and producer revenue arrangements will not be examined in detail here. Suffice it to say that the regulatory system is complicated, the board having to contend with grade and market factors on an international scale that more than rivals the sophistication of international oil markets. Fundamentally, the major preoccupation of the Wheat Board is maximizing producer returns consistent with often conflicting government policies in other areas such as feed freight assistance and the domestic pricing of bread wheats. Since its creation, the Wheat Board has proven highly effective, and, while not free from controversy, has demonstrated the long-term economic value of selective market regulations for producers and consumers alike. While much might be made of the question of whether the board has been successful in achieving the proper balance between these two groups, or promoting agrarian production efficiency, or holding back its own administrative costs, the overall gains derived by virtue of its existence are less debatable.

Obtaining a balance between consumer and producing interests will be no less difficult in the case of energy pricing than has been true of wheat. At this juncture, it is not reasonable to conclude in favour of either higher or lower overall energy prices for Canadians, let alone the ultimate effects of any pricing solution that may in future find governmental support. But, at a minimum, the solution adopted should be a studied one rather than the product of a less than full appreciation of the various interests at stake. Particular care will be required to order the difficult transition between conventional, frontier and synthetic sources of petroleum and natural gas. There are immediate difficulties that must be overcome in order to "stage in" these new, more expensive sources successfully. In the short term, the uncertainty that has centred on a domestic oil and gas pricing policy has made calculation of prospective rates of return for large energy-producing investments somewhat speculative. In partial response, the terms under which risk capital might be available were uncertain. Many large projects were either delayed or were in danger of being postponed, resulting in a forward extension of Canada's dependence upon limited conventional and/or import supplies. Bringing any single project to fruition, in the absence of a workable pricing policy, will continue to be inordinately complicated, as the Syncrude and Alaska Highway Natural Gas Pipeline experiences demonstrated. In both of these cases, special terms were necessary to ensure sufficiently attractive returns to attract financing in face of market pricing over the life of the projects.

As a particular case, Syncrude showed just how controlling the price question is in any large-scale synthetic or frontier investment. While still shrouded in controversy concerning the role of the various governments involved, the capital costs of the project, the reliability of the technology employed, and effective rates of return obtainable, Syncrude nonetheless stands as a significant reminder of the difficulties of stimulating capital investment without a timely resolution of the all-important pricing issue so basic to expected rates of return and capital market access.

The Syncrude project offered another lesson of a perhaps less obvious nature: namely, the dangers of project-specific price agreements made without the benefit of an intervening regulatory process that takes into account the specific technical and market complexities involved in a given project. The Syncrude agreement resulted from at times feverish negotiations between three governments (Alberta, Ontario and Ottawa) and the concerned private investors against a backdrop of growing public concern about the extent of Canada's oil and gas stocks and the reliability of traditional import sources. The pressures of the moment and the particular circumstances in front of each of the principals to the negotiations assumed an important role in terms of the result reached. A regulatory process that could anticipate such questions and develop predictable terms under which such issues might be resolved would be a preferable alternative from the point of view of (a) encouraging systematic frontier investments in new sources of supply, and (b) minimizing the dangers of inappropriate terms applying in individual cases.

The need to bridge the gap between lower-cost, depleting, conventional sources of hydrocarbons, and high-cost, diverse sources of energy supply in the future demands systematic control over extremely complicated and important marketing issues. Towards this end, there is value in establishing a centralized energy marketing agency with enough jurisdictional competence to address the range of considerations involved.

- *Recommendation 13:* A National Energy Marketing Commission (NEMC) should be established to fix national energy prices.

- *Recommendation 14:* The NEMC should develop and administer a blended system that specifically addresses the need to establish a pricing regime to encourage frontier and synthetic petroleum production.

- *Recommendation 15:* The NEMC should make recommendations with respect to federal-provincial export revenue-sharing.

The primary mandate of what has been here termed the "National Energy Marketing Commission" should be locating and regulating a blended energy price with regard to (a) the availability and cost of various sources of energy, (b) their importance as provincial revenue sources, (c) the effect of pricing upon the level of economic activity in the consuming markets, and (d) the pace and direction of industry reinvestment that may result from a given pricing decision. This blended price should form the basis for prices charged to consumers, making necessary adjustments for transportation cost differentials, and, in exceptional cases, for the particular exigencies of an individual market. As a rule, however, the compassion of the system should be initially directed towards the producing side of the balance, with specific source pricing based upon the real costs of production, plus federal or provincial off-takes, and, in the case of an unconnected source, the price necessary to ensure the feasibility of the initial investment (subject perhaps to later review).

As a buyer, the commission should evolve price schedules that are the product of its own negotiations with producers, the applicable federal-provincial agreements as have applied to provincially-produced crude oil, and prices as stipulated under previously agreed "new investment programs" whereby an agreed higher cost is applied to a new source of supply (at a determined price above the national average).

As a seller, the commission could attempt to maintain as simple a pricing procedure as circumstances allow. In the case of petroleum, for example, the NEP has stipulated a series of levies that will produce a blended oil price that will in effect neutralize the current differences between synthetic, domestic and import supplies. Where possible, the commission might apply an all-energy source blended average and confine the exceptions to those identified for special treatment by government. At the moment, qualifying examples under the NEP include a lower price for natural gas or other energy sources that can add to petroleum conservation through substitution.

To be effective, the commission should regulate all transactions involving international or interprovincial energy trade, except petroleum imports for which a specialized tribunal has already been proposed (see chapter 1). The commission thus would assume nationally many of the functions presently performed by the Alberta Petroleum Marketing Commission at the provincial level, but on an all-energy basis. The National Energy Marketing Commission should therefore enjoy a statutory monopoly over the full range of energy transactions, save those that are completed entirely within one province. Where provincial consent is obtained, the commission should act with delegated power to exercise similar functions with respect to intraprovincial transactions.

A tribunal such as has been described represents a fundamental departure from procedures that have governed to this point. It also clearly represents a major increase in terms of government regulation over the private economy. But in this instance, government involvement should successfully eliminate many bottlenecks restraining the pace of industry activity. Regulation as here described can perform services of critical importance by easing uncertainties that today constrain investment in new sources, including securing forward price conditions that will facilitate predictable rates of return and help secure financing. From a provincial point of view, a national marketing scheme will make it possible to determine an orderly balance between federal and provincial market-sharing and open opportunities for comprehensive revenue-sharing between the two levels of government. Finally, the National Energy Marketing Commission will provide an important informed window on a "fair energy price" for Canadian producers, consumers and taxpayers.

Appendix

State Involvement in the Oil and Gas Industries: Some Case Studies

Brazil

Petrobras — Petroleo Brasileiro Sociedade Anónima — was established in 1953 as the supervisory agent of the state monopoly of the exploration, production and refining of petroleum. Able to produce less than half the country's needs, Petrobras became the world's largest single importer of foreign oil. Rising prices in 1973 and 1974 prompted the establishment of Braspetro, a subsidiary of Petrobras, to explore for oil overseas.

In 1975, domestic exploration policy was amended to permit exploration in Brazil by foreign oil companies on a "risk contract" basis. The contractor was required to purchase surveys of all potential areas and to meet all exploration and development costs. Petrobras retained ownership in any resources discovered and would pay for discoveries, reimbursing the contractor for production expenses only with respect to "commercial" discoveries as determined by the government. Petrobras also retained supervisory control over all contractors and subcontractors. Limited response to this offer (only five bids were received) led to some revisions in the policy in 1977. The size of the exploration area was increased and the price of geological information decreased.

Although natural gas discoveries remain exclusive property of Petrobras, in the 1977 offerings gas production terms were offered. Previously there had been no remuneration for gas discovered.

Petrobras itself was involved in drilling in the Campos Basin in anticipation of a full production rate of 45,000 barrels a day from the Garoupa provisional sea floor system by 1978.

Braspetro has been involved, either on its own or in partnership in

130

foreign concessions, in discovery of oil in Iran and Algeria and of gas in Egypt, and in production in Columbia and refining in Italy. It also has interests in the Philippines, Iran and Libya.

Electric power in Brazil is under the jurisdiction of the Ministry of Mines and Energy, and is supervised by Electrobras. Hydraulic power plants, and coal, oil-fired thermal and diesel installations provide electricity through state and private concessionaires under the supervision of Electrobras.

Brazil's nuclear energy program is administered by the ministry through Nuclebras, established in 1974. Nuclebras has contracted with Westinghouse and Kraftwerk Union to provide reactors to be on line by the mid 1980s. Brazil is hoping to establish its uranium industry to the extent that it will be self-sufficient with respect to nuclear energy by 1990.

Petrochemical production is by law outside Petrobras' scope of operation and is supervised by a subsidiary, Petroquisa, which operates in joint ventures as a minority shareholder.

Brazil is planning, under the direction of Petrobras, to have completed an oil shale plant by 1983, to exploit its oil shale deposit, the second largest in the world. Projected production is 50,000 barrels of synthetic oil per day.

Other sources of energy, coal, wood or bagasse and charcoal are not subject to state supervision. These sources provide roughly 35 per cent of Brazil's energy.

Petrobras began a program of predominantly offshore drilling in 1977 in a push for self-sufficiency by 1980. Much of the drilling was done on a risk contract basis by foreign companies. By the end of 1979 the success of the project seemed marginal. The Campos permanent production system is expected to produce 300,000 bl/d by 1983. It has, however, been predicted that by the late 1980s local consumption will have risen to 1.5 million bl/d.

In 1977, it was decided that the government-owned Copesul would build a large petrochemical complex at Triunfo.

In 1980, Petrobras contracted with the West German Krupp-Koppes to design and build a coal gasification plant. Start-up is expected in 1983.

Ecuador

The Ecuadorian state oil company, CEPE (Corporación Estatal de Petrolera Ecuatoriana), was established in 1972 to have control over the country's petroleum industry. All petroleum industry in Ecuador is the property of the state and may only be exploited under the ultimate supervision of the Ministry of Natural Resources and Energy. No oil exports are permitted unless domestic needs have been met. Exact amounts needed domestically and domestic prices are set by the government.

Foreign exploration and production in Ecuador is permitted on two bases. The first is a concession granted to explore and develop a specific area. The most significant concession is that of Texaco/Gulf in the Oriente fields. CEPE has purchased an interest in the production. The second basis is the association contract, which was instituted in 1972. The contract to explore and develop an area is administered by the Administration Committee, consisting of an equal number of representatives from CEPE and the contracting company. Managerial decisions are made by the committee. In the event of a dispute, the matter is referred to the chairmen of CEPE and the contracting company. CEPE's financial involvement in association contracts may take one of two forms: either partnership, i.e., participation to a specified percentage in expenses and returns, or symbolic participation, in which CEPE receives payment of a percentage increasing as production increases. Companies are taxed on export oil on the basis of a tax reference price determined by the government rather than an actual market price. New legislation passed in 1977 permitted CEPE to offer more attractive terms to the companies, including a provision that part of the oil output would be retained by the companies to defray exploration and development costs.

CEPE began large-scale refinery operations at Esmeraldas in 1977. The refinery has a capacity of 50,000 bl/d, but was initially operated at less than full capacity due to inadequate outlets to dispose of the product. CEPE entered into an agreement in 1978 to build a pipeline linking Esmeraldas with Quito, the capital city, and to complete a shipping facility off Esmeraldas to remedy this problem. By 1980, CEPE planned to expand both the shipping outlet and the refinery to more than double the capacity.

Mexico

In 1938, all foreign oil companies operating in Mexico were nationalized by order of the then President Cárdenas. Simultaneously PEMEX — Petróloeos Mexicanos — was established to control the oil and gas industry in Mexico, including exploration and production, refining, distribution and petrochemical processing.

PEMEX is a wholly-owned public agency having authority to carry on business and hold property in its own name. Its financial policy, budget, expenditures and pricing structure are subject to government approval. It is PEMEX and not the Mexican government that has legal responsibility for obligations incurred by the company. Domestic prices are set by the government at levels which in theory will cover operating costs. Prices for export oil follow world market prices. Large discoveries of oil in the Gulf of Campeche and Chicontepec in 1977 and 1978 have more than doubled Mexico's hydrocarbon potential. PEMEX is responsible for the operation of these fields. By the end of 1978, PEMEX had entered into two crude export contracts with the United States at an estimated value of $91.4 million.

PEMEX is responsible for the refining of petroleum in Mexico. It has recently expanded its refining capacity to keep pace with demand both for domestic consumption and export. The company also has control over the transportation network for oil, gas and petrochemical feedstocks. There is a pipeline system throughout Mexico and extending into the United States for export of gas. Expansion of PEMEX's petrochemical facility at Cosoleacaque was part of a six-year plan to double refining capacity and triple petrochemical production.

Venezuela
Increased control over the petroleum industry by the Venezuelan government has been a gradual trend beginning in the mid 1930s when an Office of Hydrocarbons was established to supervise the operation of private petroleum companies which had previously been unfettered. In 1943, increased taxes and royalties, along with firmer control, were spurred by growing Venezuelan nationalism. By 1948, the tax policy was such that the government received a 50 per cent tax on any sum by which a company's net profits exceeded the government revenues from that company for that year.

A moderate policy of expropriation began in 1958. There was a profit sharing of 65/35 in favour of the state, with respect to privately-owned companies. In 1960, the Corporación Venezolana del Petróleo (CVP) was formed to deal primarily with domestic marketing of oil products. There was very little emphasis on exploration and development.

The government initiated a new series of service contracts in 1971 under which the private companies became partners of CVP. There were no further concessions, but contracts whose terms were more favourable to the government. Also in 1971 the government enacted

133

the Hydrocarbons Reversion Law, under which all concessions and property owned by the companies would revert to the state when the concessions expired. Land which had not yet been developed would revert within three years. The law also provided that government approval was required for any changes in operation, including new exploration.

At the time of the OPEC price increases in 1973-74, Venezuela, using its new-found leverage, passed a law effecting early reversion of the companies' concessions. The law was enacted in 1975 and stated that nationalization would be completed by January 1, 1976. A new national oil company was created to administer the nationalization, Petroléos de Venezuela ("Petroven" or PDV). In the initial stages of nationalization smaller companies were integrated into larger ones. PDV reduced the number of operating companies, now under new names, to fourteen by the end of 1977. The former concessionaires were paid compensation on the basis of book value of their holdings. PDV entered into four-year contracts for technological services with nine of the former concessionaires to ensure a smooth transition. PDV operates as a supervisory and planning agent over the nationalized companies. Approvals for exploration and development and refinery projects are given by PDV. Prices are set by the Ministry of Mines and Energy and tend generally to follow OPEC prices.

PDV announced a massive exploration program in 1977 involving all of the fourteen national companies. Tremendous expenditures are to be made over a ten-year period. The project is to be financed from PDV's revenues from the fourteen operating companies.

Venezuela's refineries are all owned by PDV and operated through the companies. An improvement and modernization program was approved in 1977 and begun in 1978. PDV also acquired an interest in refineries in Aruba and Curacao to increase its refining capacity. PDV's involvement in petrochemical processing is handled by its subsidiary Pequiven.

Federal Republic of Germany
West Germany's petroleum market is predominantly serviced by subsidiaries of the large multinational companies. German-owned companies account for only 20 per cent of the domestic market and refining capacity. Domestic exploration and production are dominated by German subsidiaries of multinational companies, and by privately-owned German companies. The state's involvement is limited to royalties and taxes.

134

VEBA — Vereingte Elektrizitats und Bergwerke AG — Germany's major state oil company was established in 1929 as a holding company to amalgamate Prussian holdings, at which time it had only a small interest in oil and gas. In 1973, VEBA was officially designated as the central agency of the German oil interests and as the German government's link with international oil companies. The German government owns 40 per cent of the shares in VEBA.

Having abandoned an attempt in 1964 to encourage domestic production through a tariff on imports, which violated EEC rules, the government turned to a subsidy scheme for domestic production to reduce reliance on imported oil.

In 1974 a wholly-owned subsidiary of VEBA, VEBA Chemie purchased 96.1 per cent of the stock in Gelsenberg, a private German oil company operating on the international level. Following this acquisition, VEBA and its associates control about 19 per cent of Germany's refining capacity, the largest share controlled by any company in the country. VEBA also controls through its 56 per cent holding in ARAL, a large share of the gasoline distribution market, roughly 25 per cent.

VEBA is also involved in exploration projects for which it has received substantial government subsidies. These subsidies are partly repayable if and when discoveries are made. VEBA's exploration involvement is mainly through its 56 per cent holding in Deminex, an international exploration group composed of many of Germany's oil companies. Deminex and its partners have exploration interests in roughly a dozen European countries and more than twenty countries outside Europe.

Domestic production of natural gas is handled by private companies, receiving government support in the form of market guarantees. Imports of gas must be licensed by the government. There are currently contracts to import from the Netherlands, the Soviet Union and Norway. German companies have also entered into a 20-year contract with Algeria's Sonatrach to import liquified natural gas. VEBA has a 28 per cent ownership in Ruhrgas, West Germany's largest gas importer and distributor. In 1978, the German government refused to permit BP to purchase more than 9 per cent of VEBA's shares, in order to prevent foreign ownership of Ruhrgas from exceeding 49.9 per cent.

The Netherlands
The petroleum industry in the Netherlands consists largely of gas production and export, and the refining of oil imports.

Legislation passed in 1976, with respect to licensing production of oil and gas, requires that the state have 50 per cent participation in any domestic production. The state oil company which supervises production is DSM — Dutch State Mines. The licences are granted for a 10-year term, with the requirement that 50 per cent of the exploration area be relinquished at the end of the sixth year. The government exacts a 70 per cent tax on net profits, granting some relief for fields with very high production costs, as an incentive to develop higher risk areas. Prior to the passage of this new legislation, licences were of a 15-year duration. The relinquishment took place at the end of the tenth year. Only a 40 per cent government involvement was required in gas production, and government taxes were only 50 per cent.

The first major gas find in 1959 at Gröningen is still producing most of the Netherlands gas. It is operated by NAM (Nederlandse Aardolie Maatschappij, which is owned 50 per cent by Exxon and 50 per cent by a subsidiary of Royal Dutch-Shell) and by DSM which has a 40 per cent interest. Gas marketing and distribution in the Netherlands is handled by Gasunie. DSM owns 40 per cent of the shares. The state has a 10 per cent direct interest. Exports of gas are managed by NAM Gas Export, a subsidiary of NAM, which has no government participation.

Imports of gas will be required to meet a short-fall. Gasunie has contracted with Sonatrach of Algeria to import liquified natural gas. The expected short-fall is the result in a change of policy regarding gas exports. In 1976, it was announced that there would be no renewal of export contracts and no new contracts entered into unless new reserves were discovered. The Gröningen field was to be conserved for future domestic consumption.

The refining industry is a major part of the Netherlands oil industry. It is dominated by the major multinational oil companies. Most of the product that is refined in the Netherlands is imported through Rotterdam and immediately exported. Marketing of gasoline within the Netherlands is also dominated by the seven major multinationals which all have their own distribution networks of retail outlets.

In 1975, DSM was reorganized to permit it to participate in petrochemical production. DSM acquired a 25 per cent interest in Limagas, a distribution company, and a 10 per cent interest in Ultra-Centrifuge Nederland, a uranium enrichment operation, to obtain raw materials for use in petrochemical processes. In 1979, DSM began building an ethylene plant in South Limburg.

Malaysia

Prior to 1974 Malaysia's oil industry was operated entirely by private companies. Concessions were granted on a 50/50 profit-sharing basis with the government. In 1974, new legislation was enacted establishing Petronas as the national petroleum company. The legislation provided for a six-month period during which all outstanding concessions were to be converted to production-sharing agreements, similar to the Indonesian agreements. The government plans that Petronas will eventually assume full ownership over all oil and gas, and rights to all production thereof, including petrochemical processing. The government regulates pricing of oil and gas in Malaysia by setting a base price from which the profit split is calculated.

Petronas was given the legal right to require that the companies entering into the agreements sell a certain portion of management shares to Petronas. There was substantial opposition from the companies, delaying negotiation of the agreements, and the right has not been enforced.

In 1977, Petronas entered into an agreement to export liquified natural gas to Japan. Petronas has a 65 per cent interest in this project, its partners being Shell and Mitsubishi. Work on the export chain was begun in 1980. Exports are scheduled to begin in 1983.

Petronas Carigali was established in 1978 as the exploration arm of Petronas, to do exploration and to act as a partner in future offshore production. Petronas Carigali began to drill in 1979, without a partner, in the Sotong discovery which had been relinquished by Conoco when negotiations between Conoco and Petronas broke down. Petronas Carigali is developing the discovery.

Notes

Chapter 1: Canadian Import Requirements and the International Petroleum Market

[1] Depletion offset is defined as the quantity that must be discovered to replace the amount produced in a given period, assuming producibility between old and new reserves to be constant.

[2] A good example for the extensive lead time necessary between project conception and birth can be found in Canada's northern pipeline debate, which had its beginnings with the proposed Mackenzie Valley natural gas pipeline which was first seriously considered in 1971. It was not finally disposed of as an option until 1977, when approval was given to the Alcan "alternative." The Alcan project is not at best slated for completion until 1986-87. Even allowing for more expeditious regulatory treatment of a northern pipeline or other large-scale energy project, it is . difficult to imagine resolution of the many logistical obstacles involved in anything less than a decade.

[3] Estimates of total Canadian requirements are varied. Energy, Mines and Resources Canada has at various times advanced a figure of $200 billion. The Royal Bank was recently quoted as having estimated that about $1.4 trillion would be necessary for Canadian energy projects over the next two decades. What is perfectly clear is that by anyone's standards the capital requirements of Canadian energy self-sufficiency will be immense. Indeed they are substantial to the point that there are serious doubts as to whether or not Canada can in fact develop needed supplies.

[4] *International Petroleum Encyclopaedia, 1978* (Tulsa, Oklahoma: The Petroleum Publishing Co., 1978).

[5] National Energy Board, *Canadian Oil: Supply and Requirements* (September 1975).

[6] Energy, Mines and Resources Canada, Energy Strategy Branch, *Canadian Oil and Gas Supply Demand Overview* (November 1979).

[7] For a summary of IEA estimates see *Oil and Energy Trends*, vol. 4, no. 8 (August 17, 1979), p. 8 (published by Energy Economics Research Ltd., U.K.).

[8] The preference for development of indigenous supplies favours all forms of substitute energy and not only domestic oil potential. Indeed some nations, the United States most notably, allowed substantial reserves of petroleum and natural gas to build up and remain capped while imports from Canada and the world market were favoured. See Cabinet Task Force on Oil Imports Control, *The Oil Import Question: A Report on the Relationship of Oil Imports to the National Security* (Washington D.C.: U.S. Govt. Printing Office, February 1970).

[9] See John Davis, *Canadian Energy Prospects*, Royal Commission on Canada's Economic Prospects (March 1957).

[10] This was a major preoccupation of both the producing industry and the government of Alberta. See William Kilbourn, *Pipeline: Trans Canada and the Great Debate: A History of Business and Politics* (Toronto: Clarke Irwin, 1970), and the Province of Alberta Natural Gas Commission, *Enquiry into Reserves and Consumption of Natural Gas in the Province of Alberta: A Report of the Commission* (1948).

[11] Royal Commission on Energy, *2nd Report* (July 1959), pp. 50-51.

[12] Cabinet Task Force, *The Oil Import Question*.

[13] Anthony Sampson, *The Seven Sisters: The Great Oil Companies and the World They Shaped* (New York: Viking Press, 1975).

[14] Most detailed histories readily acknowledge that the extent of collusion between the Seven Sisters has been rather exaggerated. In lieu of direct contact a certain amount of shared interest has acted as an effective moderator of the competitive urge. But at the marketing end of the industry there has been a substantial amount of competitive pressure. At the exploratory/development end this has been true in some areas, most particularly North America, but elsewhere monopoly concessions were at one time the rule.

[15] As Sampson pointed out, the Seven Sisters have historically proved to be highly dependent upon the aid and diplomatic clout of the Western governments and if anything were in fear of the political controversy generated by the OPEC embargo and price increases.

[16] See Cabinet Task Force, *The Oil Import Question*.

[17] Walter Levy, "Oil and the Decline of the West," *Foreign Affairs*, Summer 1980, p. 999.

[18] VLCC or Very Large Crude Carrier refers to tankers of 160,000 deadweight tons and above. ULCC or Ultra Large Crude Carrier refers to tankers of 200,000 deadweight tons and above.

[19] Some illustration of the general trend towards larger and larger tankers can be seen in the reported 1979 tankers orders which, according to the *International Petroleum Encyclopaedia*, range from between 600,000 dwt. to a low of 150,000 dwt. Equally, a review of world tanker ports reveals that the major petroleum exporters all have facilities designed to accommodate VLCC and ULCC traffic. It is also noteworthy that Suez tanker traffic has been so reduced as to cause Egypt to implement a discriminatory tariff structure in an attempt to entice more small tankers. See the *Globe and Mail*, October 17, 1980, p. B3.

[20] Egypt has begun to realize some of its oil-producing potential. In 1979, Egypt oil flows topped 500,000 barrels per day, and by mid 1982 a number of plays were the subject of exploratory activity. Notwithstanding the domestic economic importance of more oil production, the prospects for Egypt reaching world-scale producing status are thought to be slim at the present time.

[21] OPEC was first formed in 1961 as a result of a summit held at Caracas, Venezuela. The original membership included Iran, Iraq, Kuwait, Saudi Arabia and Venezuela.

[22] See Sampson, *The Seven Sisters*, and Fariborz Ghadar, *The Evolution of OPEC Strategy* (Lexington, Mass.: Lexington Books/D.C. Heath, 1977).

[23] See, for example, William M. Brown and Herman Kahn, "Why OPEC is Vulnerable," *Fortune*, July 14, 1980, p. 66.

[24] "Cartel — a combination of producers of any product joined together to control its production, sales, and price, and to obtain a monopoly in any particular industry or

commodity.'' *Black's Law Dictionary*, revised 4th edition (St. Paul, Minn.: West Publishing Co., 1968), p. 270.

[25] ''The principal aim of the organization shall be the coordination and unification of the petroleum policies of member countries and the determination of the best means for safeguarding their interests, individually and collectively.'' The charter further provided that ''The organization shall devise ways and means of ensuring the stabilization of prices in international markets with a view to eliminating harmful and unnecessary fluctuations.'' *International Petroleum Encyclopaedia, 1978.*

[26] OPEC's negotiations immediately following the Iranian Revolution were unsuccessful in reaching a consensus on a posted price as a result of extreme upward pressure arising from the strong spot market. The acquiescence of member nations to a ''split'' was in part owing to the increased volume of oil traffic through the informal market, thus allowing for maintained revenue for most countries despite the sale of crude at lower prices to the established customers of Saudi Arabia.

[27] The spot market has historically accounted for anywhere between 3 and 15 per cent of the total annual global petroleum sales of OPEC. While it is true that the conditions prevailing in the spot market are generally symptomatic of worldwide demand and supply trends, there has nonetheless been a tendency to overstate the significance of periodic gluts. The most recent glut occurred in response to excessive purchasing immediately following the Iranian Revolution. A number of nations, most notably Japan, attempted to build up domestic stocks rapidly in face of possible additional disruptions. The spot market was thus at an all-time high in terms of volume, with prices also approaching record levels. As storage facilities were filled, the level of spot purchases was accordingly reduced and conditions in the market began to soften. Minor variations in demand patterns had an additional effect during the summer of 1980, with American needs in particular proving to be lower than anticipated. The glut, however, is not symptomatic of excess production or a worldwide surplus that will have a persistent impact in terms of the balance between demand and supply. It is instead a decidedly temporary condition without great meaning in terms of the overall direction of demand and supply.

[28] The historical use by Iran of the spot market is a good case in point. The Shah of Iran was one of the most willing to capitalize upon spot market opportunities at a fairly early stage. More recently a great percentage of Iranian oil was sold on the spot market, with Iran at one point contending that it would move all its oil in this way. That country's attitude towards the spot market has recently been revised somewhat in face of the softening of the spot price. It is, however, not unreasonable to assume that, as time progresses, more and more use will be made of spot contracts by Iranian and other Middle East producers.

[29] As discussed below, oil in the ground is a highly lucrative investment and possibly the safest available inflationary hedge. Doubts over total resource strength and limited potential for economic diversification have in some instances caused changes to production targets. This concern will undoubtedly spread to other nations.

[30] The current members of OPEC are Algeria, Ecuador, Gabon, Indonesia, Iran, Iraq, Kuwait, Libya, Nigeria, Qatar, Saudi Arabia, The United Arab Emirates and Venezuela. The members of the Organization of Arab Petroleum Exporting countries (OAPEC) are Algeria, Bahrain, Egypt, Iraq, Kuwait, Libya, Saudi Arabia, Syria and The United Arab Emirates. Bahrain, Egypt and Syria, as small petroleum producers, are not members of OPEC.

[31] Exxon, *World Energy Outlook* (1979).

140

32 See Organization for Economic Cooperation and Development, *Energy Conservation in the International Energy Agency* (Paris, 1976).

33 USSR production for 1978 was estimated to be 11,400,000 bl/d, as opposed to U.S. production of 8,660,000 bl/d and Saudi Arabia's 7,800,000 bl/d for the same period.

34 91,000 x 10^9 cubic feet estimated as of 1979.

35 Petroleum imports in 1979 alone amounted to $6 billions in foreign exchange.

36 Such sales totalled 129 million barrels in 1979.

37 According to the CIA, Soviet oil and gas equipment and technology orders from the West totalled roughly $3.1 billion (exclusive of large diameter pipeline orders) for the period 1972-76. See Central Intelligence Agency, *Prospects for Soviet Oil Production: A Supplemental Analysis* (July 1977), p. 27.

38 The USSR supplies 75 per cent of the oil needs of the Eastern European Communist bloc. See Central Intelligence Agency, *Prospects for Soviet Oil Production* (April 1977), p. 8.

39 The *Oil and Gas Journal* year-end estimates have begun to show an apparent downward trend in the rate of production increments: 1979 (projected) — 432,000 bl/d; 1978 — 512,000 bl/d; 1977 — 522,000 bl/d; 1976 — 578,000 bl/d; 1975 — 637,000 bl/d.

40 According to press reports, Soviet oil prices were increased approximately 100 per cent in 1978. See the *Globe and Mail*, March 2, 1978, p. 11.

41 CIA, *Prospects for Soviet Oil Production*.

42 Water flooding is a common practice in the Soviet Union to boost well flows through augmentation of formation pressure. Damage to reservoirs and consequent lowering of production/recovery prospects is quite widespread in some of the major producing regions of the country.

43 CIA, *Prospects for Soviet Oil Production: A Supplemental Analysis*.

44 Over the period 1971-75 the USSR drilled a total of 2 million metres. In 1975 the U.S. drilled 3 million metres. Both nations had roughly 1600-1700 rigs in use during this period.

45 Much of the available evidence relating to Soviet field production problems is by way of derivative inference, compiled on the strength of Western sales of production equipment in general, and of submersible pumping equipment in particular. The West's technical lead in this respect is unrivalled. Thus total USSR imports provide what is thought to be a quite accurate indication of the dimension of Soviet production difficulties. On this basis the Soviet dilemma appears very substantial in the short run and probably insurmountable over the medium term as rapid rates of production decline begin to establish themselves firmly in the country's major producing centres.

46 The main export facility, IGAT I (Iranian Gas Trunkline), can export 900 million cubic feet a day. Flow was interrupted twice in 1978, the first occasion because of corrosion, the second occasion for political reasons. As of 1981 a partially completed second facility (IGAT II) has been cancelled. This U.S. $2.4 billion, 56-inch line was to move an additional 660 billion cubic feet a year to the USSR which planned in turn to export an equal amount to West Germany, France, Austria and Czechoslovakia. IGAT I flows over 1979 were reportedly less than 450 million cubic feet a day.

47 In 1978 selling prices were reported to be three times the purchase price of Iran's gas. *International Petroleum Encyclopaedia, 1980* (Tulsa, Oklahoma: The

Petroleum Publishing Co., 1980), p. 184.

[48] Even if Soviet requirements can continue to be met with indigenous supplies, the rate of growth of consumption among its Eastern European satellites has approached 8 per cent per year. If this rate of growth is to continue, access to OPEC production may be necessary.

[49] See Wolfgang Sassin, "Energy," *Scientific American*, September 1980.

[50] Saudi Arabia and Kuwait have both reportedly insisted that the oil companies forced to reduce their contract deliveries maintain flows to LDCs at their full level. Concession terms under which LDCs acquire oil include a variety of devices "other than direct discounts." See "OPEC's Current Thinking," *Petroleum Economist*, December 1979, pp. 498-99.

[51] Sassin, "Energy."

[52] Ibid. See also *International Petroleum Encyclopaedia, 1980*, pp. 212-16.

[53] Landsat 2 Earth Resources Satellite.

[54] Remaining reserves are below five times the current U.S. annual consumption level (1979 crude reserves = 27.8 billion barrels. Total annual consumption for 1979 = 17.7 million bl/d. Reserve life index = 4.303).

[55] There are several examples. The most notable is Iraq. Prior to the Iraqi-Iranian war, Iraq's production was deliberately held to roughly 65 per cent of its capacity. Exploration activity has also been restrained.

[56] The seizure of the sacred Mosque at Mecca by religious zealots on November 20, 1979, in the wake of the Iranian Revolution and the increased force of Islamic fundamentalism reportedly have had a sobering influence upon the Saudis' development planning.

[57] Legislative restrictions with respect to foreign ownership impose large limits upon overseas investment opportunities for the OPEC nations, further exacerbating the imbalances.

[58] "Although Saudi Arabia has the reserve potential to meet increased demand between now and 1985, we doubt the Saudis will be able, or willing, to do so. . . Wanting to conserve their valuable resource and having no immediate need for more money, the Saudis have no economic incentive to expand production." U.S. Central Intelligence Agency, *The International Energy Situation: Outlook to 1985* (April 1977).

[59] U.S. relations with Iran (under the late Shah) and with Saudi Arabia are two excellent cases in point.

[60] Levy, "Oil and the Decline of the West," p. 1009.

[61] Venezuela, after the announced reductions of 1978, increased production in response to the Iran cutbacks of early 1979. Production cutbacks in response to the declining life index will be resumed in 1980-81 if current government programs are adhered to.

[62] Total Saudis reserves were estimated to be 165.7 billion barrels proved for the year-end 1978.

[63] Kuwait in fact cut sales to the Japanese-owned Arabian Oil Co. from 900,000 bl/d to 234,000 bl/d in 1979, citing concern over production lands. Oman's production over the same period was down about 8 per cent.

[64] One of the most impressive projects in this regard was the Abadan refining complex (now destroyed) which was designed to service domestic market requirements to the tune of 60 per cent of its output. The remaining 40 per cent was to be taken up with product exports, although marketing and political problems plagued this end of the operation.

142

[65] Pricing was also under the control of the multinationals. Indeed it is commonly said that OPEC's very formation was the product of a decision by Monroe Rathbone to cut the posted price by an average of 10 cents a barrel in August 1960 on top of the 8-cent cut of a year before. The income losses for the Middle East producers were such as to guarantee concerted extreme action. See Sampson, *The Seven Sisters*, chapter 8.

[66] In some cases elaborate off-take commitments were in effect among producers which allowed the multinationals to control national output. These were in force in both Iran and Saudi Arabia before 1960 and in effect governed production decisions.

[67] "Oil Shortages Could Add to Eastern Europe Unrest," *The Asian Wall Street Journal*, November 6, 1980, p. 6.

[68] Preamble, Agreement on International Energy Program, IEA/SEQ (76) 30.

[69] Ibid.

[70] Ibid.

[71] Ibid, article 2(2).

[72] Ibid, chapter II, article 14.

[73] Ibid, articles 13, 14, 7, 9, 10 and 11.

[74] Ibid, articles 17, 8, 9, 10, and 11.

[75] See Henry Kissinger, *The White House Years* (Boston: Little, Brown, 1978).

[76] W. Levy, "A Warning to the Oil Consuming Nations," *Fortune*, May 21, 1979, p. 48.

[77] See Central Intelligence Agency, National Foreign Assessment Centre, *International Energy Statistical Review*, June 24, 1980, and OECD International Energy Agency, *Quarterly Oil Statistics, Fourth Quarter 1979* (1980/No. 1).

[78] Davis, *Canadian Energy Prospects*, p. 50.

[79] A.P. Bell.

[80] "Imperial Oil Claims Diversion Run on International Guidelines," *Globe and Mail*, February 22, 1979, p. B1.

[81] The proverbial "high water mark" in this regard is perhaps to be found in the National Energy Board's oil supply analysis of October 1974 where it was contended that "Concerning oil sands and heavy crude reserves, the Board currently accepts the general consensus that a reasonable addition rate would be one mining extraction plant every two years under likely economic, environmental, material and labour supply conditions. It is also probable that two in-situ plants might be on stream in the mid to late 1980s." National Energy Board, "In the Matter of the Exportation of Oil," Report to the Honourable Minister of Energy, Mines and Resources (October 1974), pp. 2-3.

[82] As of August 1980 the breakdown by source of Canadian import supplies was as follows: Venezuela — 38.8%; Africa — 2.9%; other western hemisphere — 1.2%; Saudi Arabia — 47.2%; other Middle East — 12.4%; other — 1.5%. As a general trend, Venezuela imports are in decline, being offset by increased volumes from Middle East sources.

[83] Exxon directed Imperial to divert 25,000 bl/d of Venezuela crude to the U.S. Atlantic seaboard to offset the effect of the announced reduction in crude sales upon that market. The flurry of negotiations that followed saw the diversions made, but held to between 8,000 and 9,000 bl/d.

[84] The evidence raised before the Nova Scotia Public Utilities Board in 1974 with respect to the use made by Exxon of dummy subsidiary corporations such as Albury in Bermuda to effect maximum pricing of international crude movements implies a rather strong need to police such transactions. But the need to police should not be

143

understood as a total condemnation of marketing systems which, by virtue of their enormous size and complexity alone, offer large advantages to their customers.

[85] During the Imperial Oil-Ottawa debate over the allocation of Venezuela output reductions, Ottawa was concerned about the possibility of contracted oil being replaced by more costly supplies purchased on the spot market. In an effort to offset this possibility, the Oil Import Compensation Board was directed to reject invoices from Imperial that might reflect spot rates.

[86] As the post-Iranian Revolution movement of spot prices demonstrated, conditions within the international petroleum market can vary rapidly between extremes. The total volume of available world storage is in this sense the upper constraint with respect to continued upward speculative pressure. The initial price stability that was retained despite the Iranian-Iraqi war was the product of topped-up world storages, which effectively capped the capacity of the market to engage in panic buying. By contrast, the drawdown of storages following the 1978 Iranian Revolution allowed full play to be given to the panic felt by the consuming nations. International prices shot up accordingly at an alarming rate and persisted until more or less all of these storage facilities were employed.

Chapter 2: Federal Regulation of Energy

[1] *The National Energy Program 1980* (Ottawa: Energy, Mines and Resources Canada, 1980), p. 93.

[2] Ibid, p. 93.

[3] Ibid.

[4] Ibid, p. 98.

[5] See, for example, Amory Lovins, *World Energy Strategies: Facts, Issues and Options* (Cambridge, Mass.: Ballinger Publishing, 1975).

[6] The Petro-Canada Act, S.C. 1974-75, c. 61.

[7] *National Energy Program*, p. 99.

[8] *International Petroleum Intelligence Weekly*, February 10, 1981.

[9] *National Energy Program*, p. 25.

[10] Ibid, p. 54.

[11] Ibid, p. 53 and passim.

[12] Ibid, pp. 98-99.

[13] Ibid, p. 101.

[14] Ibid, p. 87.

[15] Ibid, p. 100.

[16] Ibid.

[17] Ibid.

[18] Energy, Mines and Resources, *Canadian Oil and Gas Supply/Demand Overview*, (Ottawa, November 1979), Figure 25, p. 61.

[19] This includes propane, butane and ethane.

[20] *National Energy Program*, p. 63.

[21] Ibid.

[22] Ibid.

[23] Ibid, p. 101.

[24] Ibid.

[25] Ibid.

[26] See EMR, *Canadian Oil and Gas Supply/Demand Overview*, Table 22, p. 71.

[27] Ibid.

[28] *National Energy Program*, pp. 100-101.

[29] Ibid, p. 101.

[30] National Energy Board, *Canadian Natural Gas: Supply and Requirements* (Ottawa, 1979).

[31] See, for example, "Petrochemical Industry Struggles to Interpret NEP Pronouncement," *Energy Analects*, vol. 10, no. 3 (January 30, 1981).

[32] Bruce F. Willson, *The Energy Squeeze: Canadian Policies for Survival* (Toronto: Canadian Institute for Economic Policy/James Lorimer & Co., 1980).

[33] National Energy Board, *Reasons for Decision* (November 1979).

[34] The Conference Board of Canada, *Annual Report, 1980.*

[35] Alberta has 8.25 per cent of the country's total population and contributes 12 per cent of total general revenue.

[36] To take two examples, TransCanada Pipelines has paid no income tax since its creation. Shell Canada in the fiscal period ending 1979 paid no federal income tax.

[37] *National Energy Program*, p. 35.

[38] Ibid.

[39] Ibid, p. 112.

[40] Ibid.

[41] Suppose a $1,000 investment is made. Under this system, on wells in excess of $5 million the investor could claim a Canadian Exploration Expense (CEE) of 100 per cent or $1,000, an Earned Depletion Allowance (EDA) of 33⅓ per cent or $333.33, and a Frontier Exploration Allowance (FEA) of 66⅔ per cent or $666.66 to yield a total of $2,000 or 200 per cent.

[42] Model (standard form) Production Sharing Agreement between Pertamina and private contractors.

[43] Of the Seven Sisters, five are U.S. companies (Exxon, Mobil, Socal, Gulf and Texaco).

[44] See discussion below.

[45] See, *Budget November 1974, Special Release* (Toronto: Richard DeBoo Ltd., November 18, 1974).

[46] *National Energy Program*, p. 39.

[47] ". . .the Government of Canada has promised to provide a replacement for the former 'super-depletion' allowance for frontier exploration which expired on April 1, 1980." Ibid, p. 39.

[48] Ibid.

[49] Following the NEP's introduction there was a flood of cancellations of exploratory programs and tarsands investments.

[50] See Rowland J. Harrison, "The Off-Shore Mineral Resources Agreement in the Maritime Provinces (1977-78)," *Dalhousie Law Journal*, vol. 4, p. 245.

[51] *National Energy Program*, p. 43.

[52] Ibid, p. 47.

[53] Ibid, p. 69 and passim.

[54] Ibid, p. 73.

[55] Ibid, p. 69.

[56] Ibid, p. 82.

[57] Ibid, p. 42.

[58] Saskatchewan Light and Power. See Ian McDougall, "Future Canadian Gas Requirements: Whether Upgraded Deliverability or Rapid Frontier Development" (Submission to the National Energy Board, Ottawa, 1975).

[59] See, for example, *Energy Analects*, vol. 10, no. 3 (January 30, 1981), p. 1.

[60] See McDougall, "Future Canadian Gas Requirements."

Chapter 3: Federal Regulatory Controls

[1] *The National Energy Program 1980* (Ottawa: Energy, Mines and Resources Canada, 1980), p. 111. "Surprise free" refers to the predicted cost trends of international oil.

[2] T.J. Courchene, *Energy and Equalization,* vol. 1, *Energy Policies for the 1980's: An Economic Analysis* (Toronto: Ontario Economic Council, 1980).

[3] Ibid.

[4] Ibid.

[5] Fiscal Arrangements Act, R.S.C. 1977, c. 258.

[6] Courchene, *Energy and Equalization,* vol. 1.

[7] In 1978 it was proposed that any province whose per capita income levels had been in excess of the national average for three consecutive years (or in other words the province of Ontario) would be ineligible.

[8] See G. Young, *Federal-Provincial Grants and Equalization: Intergovernmental Relations* (Toronto: Ontario Economic Council, 1977).

[9] Petroleum Administration Act, S.C. 1974-75-76, c. 47.

[10] Kathy Greiner, "What Price for What Oil?" *Canadian Petroleum,* December 1979, pp. 28-30.

[11] "Gulf Ties Oil Shipment to Compensation Rates," *Globe and Mail*, June 21, 1979, p. B3.

[12] *Nickel's Daily Oil Bulletin*, June 29, 1979, p. 3.

[13] Flat Rate Compensation Determination: Efficient Crude Import C's at Montreal − Equivalent Cdn. C. at Toronto = Base Compensation.

[14] *Energy Update's Oil and Gas Statistics*, January 1979, June 1979 and July 1980.

[15] Press release, Office of the Minister, Energy, Mines and Resources Canada, July 11, 1980.

[16] *National Energy Program*, p. 25.

[17] Ibid, p. 24.

[18] Royal Commission on Energy, *First Report* (Ottawa: Queen's Printer, 1959).

[19] The National Energy Board Act, R.S.C. 1970, chapter N-6 as amended.

[20] Ibid, section 3(2).

[21] Ibid, section 3(5).

[22] See Ian McDougall, "The National Energy Board," *Alberta Law Review*, vol. XI, no. 2 (1973).

[23] Gibbs et al., "A Review of the National Energy Board Policies and Practices and Recent Hearings," *Alberta Law Review*, vol. IX, no. 1 (1971).

[24] The National Energy Board Act, section 2.

[25] Ibid, section 46(1), subject of course to the Governor-in-Council's approval.

[26] Ibid, section 44.

[27] Ibid, section 55.

[28] Ibid, section 81.

[29] See discussion below concerning the 1971 acknowledgement of a foreseeable deficit in natural gas supplies, and the 1974 Gas Supply and Requirements hearings.

[30] See, for example, the estimates considered by the board during the 1969 omnibus export hearings summarized in its "Reasons for Decision," August 1969.

[31] NEB hearing Order GH-1-76.

[32] National Energy Board, *Reasons for Decision, Northern Pipeline Hearings,* 3 vols. (Ottawa: Queen's Printer, 1976).

[33] See National Energy Board, *Natural Gas Supply and Requirements* (Ottawa: Queen's Printer, 1978).

Chapter 4:   A National Energy Marketing Commission?

[1] Economic Council of Canada, *Responsible Regulation,* Interim Report of the Regulation Reference (Ottawa: Minister of Supply and Services, 1979), p. 23.

[2] British North America Act, section 91(2).

[3] Ibid, section 91 preamble.

[4] *Citizens' Insurance Co.* v. *Parsons* (1881) 7 App. C05.96, p. 113.

[5] *A.G. Canada* v. *A.G. Alberta (Insurance)* (1916) 1 A.C. 588, and *A.G. Ontario* v. *Reciprocal Insurers* (1924) A.C. 328. See also, *Re Insurance Act of Canada* (1932) A.C. 41.

[6] *Re Board of Commerce Act, 1919 and Combines and Fair Prices Act, 1919* (1922) 1 A.C. 191.

[7] See Peter Hogg, *Constitutional Law of Canada* (Toronto: Carswell, 1977), pp. 267-68.

[8] *Ontario Farm Products Marketing Reference* (1957) S.C.R. 198.

[9] *Murphy* v. *Canadian Pacific Railway* (1958) S.C.R. 626.

[10] *R.* v. *Klassen* (1959) 20 D.L.R. (2d) 406.

[11] Bora Laskin (1959) 37 *Canadian Bar Review* 63, p. 270.

[12] Ibid.

[13] *Caloil* v. *A.G. Canada* (1971) S.C.R. 543.

[14] Ibid, 551.

[15] *Anti-Inflation Reference* (1976) 2 S.C.R. 373.

[16] *A.G. Manitoba* v. *Manitoba Egg and Poultry Association* (1971) S.C.R. 689.

[17] See Hogg, *Constitutional Law of Canada,* pp. 210-11.

[18] Gerald LeDain, "Sir Lyman Duff and the Constitution" (1974) 12 *OHLJ* 261, pp. 292-93.

[19] *Russell* v. *R.* (1882) 7 App. Ca 829.

[20] *A.G. Ontario* v. *A.G. Canada (Local Prohibition)* (1896) A.C. 348.

[21] The problem here of course relates to the support available to legislative measures to prevent the occurrence of emergencies as opposed to those measures adopted ex post facto.

[22] *A.G. Ontario* v. *Canada Temperance Federation* (1946) A.C. 193.

[23] See Hogg, *Constitutional Law of Canada,* pp. 259-60.

[24] W.R. Lederman (1975) 53 *Canadian Bar Review* 597.

[25] Professor Lederman advanced this view before the Supreme Court in the *Anti-Inflation Reference.*

[26] Section 109 reads:

All Lands, Mines, Minerals and Royalties belonging to the several Provinces of Canada, Nova Scotia and New Brunswick at the Union, and all sums then due or payable for such Lands, Mines, Minerals or Royalties, shall belong to the several Provinces of Ontario, Quebec, Nova Scotia, and New Brunswick in which the same are situate or arise, subject to any Trusts existing in respect thereof and to any Interest other than that of the Province in the same.

Section 92(5) reads:

In each Province the Legislature may exclusively make laws in relation to matters coming within the classes of subject next hereinafter enunciated; that is to say — (5) The management and sale of Public Lands.

The Canadian Institute for Economic Policy Series

The Monetarist Counter-Revolution: A Critique of Canadian Monetary Policy 1975-1979
Arthur W. Donner and Douglas D. Peters

Canada's Crippled Dollar: An Analysis of International Trade and Our Troubled Balance of Payments
H. Lukin Robinson

Unemployment and Inflation: The Canadian Experience
Clarence L. Barber and John C.P. McCallum

How Ottawa Decides: Planning and Industrial Policy-Making 1968-1980
Richard D. French

Energy and Industry: The Potential of Energy Development Projects for Canadian Industry in the Eighties
Barry Beale

The Energy Squeeze: Canadian Policies for Survival
Bruce F. Willson

The Post-Keynesian Debate: A Review of Three Recent Canadian Contributions
Myron J. Gordon

Water: The Emerging Crisis in Canada
Harold D. Foster and W.R. Derrick Sewell

The Working Poor: Wage Earners and the Failure of Income Security Policies
David P. Ross

Beyond the Monetarists: Post-Keynesian Alternatives to Rampant Inflation, Low Growth and High Unemployment
Edited by David Crane

The Splintered Market: Barriers to Interprovincial Trade in Canadian Agriculture
R.E. Haack, D.R. Hughes and R.G. Shapiro

The Drug Industry: A Case Study of the Effects of Foreign Control on the Canadian Economy
Myron J. Gordon and David J. Fowler

The New Protectionism: Non-Tariff Barriers and Their Effects on Canada
Fred Lazar

Industrial Development and the Atlantic Fishery: Opportunities for Manufacturing and Skilled Workers in the 1980s
Donald J. Patton

Canada's Population Outlook: Demographic Futures and Economic Challenges
David K. Foot

Financing the Future: Canada's Capital Markets in the Eighties
Arthur W. Donner

Controlling Inflation: Learning from Experience in Canada, Europe and Japan
Clarence L. Barber and John C.P. McCallum

Canada and the Reagan Challenge: Crisis in the Canadian-American Relationship
Stephen Clarkson

The Future of Canada's Auto Industry: The Big Three and the Japanese Challenge
Ross Perry

Canadian Manufacturing: A Study of Productivity and Technological Change
Volume I: Sector Performance and Industrial Strategy
Volume II: Industry Studies 1946-1977
Uri Zohar

Canada's Cultural Industries: Broadcasting, Publishing, Records and Film
Paul Audley

Canada's Video Revolution: Home Video, Pay-TV and Beyond
Peter Lyman

The above titles are available from:

James Lorimer & Company, Publishers
Egerton Ryerson Memorial Building
35 Britain Street
Toronto, Ontario M5A 1R7